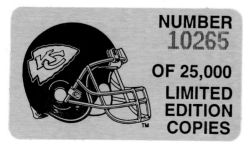

ARROWHEAD
HOME OF THE
CHIEFS

by Michael McKenzie
Foreword by Lamar Hunt

ADDAX
PUBLISHING
GROUP

Bob Snodgrass
Publisher

Gary Carson
Photo Editor

Greg Echlin
Managing Editor

Brad Breon
Publishing Consultant

Darcie Kidson
Publicity

Denny Trease
David Power
Patrons

Randy Breeden
Art Direction/Design

Dust jacket and soft cover design by Jerry Hirt

Production Assistants: Michelle Washington,
Sharon Snodgrass, Chip Power, David Power,
Jeremy Styno, Renee Van Landingham

Contributing Photographers: Hank Young,
Chris Dennis, Tim Umphrey, Kate Umphrey,
Vernon Biever, Thomas Mitchell, Dale Lightfoot,
Gary Carson, Kris-Ann McKenzie

*Select photos courtesy of the Kansas City
Chiefs.*

Published by Addax Publishing Group, Lenexa, Kansas
Printed and bound in Canada

Distributed to the trade by Andrews & McMeel,
4520 Main Street, Kansas City, Missouri 64111

Library of Congress Cataloging-in-Publication Data
McKenzie, Michael, 1945-
Arrowhead : Home of the Chiefs / by Michael McKenzie ;
foreword by
Lamar Hunt.
p. cm.
ISBN 1-886110-11-5 (limited ed., hard). – ISBN 1-886110-12-3
(general ed., pbk.). – ISBN 1-886110-36-0 (collectors ed.,
leather)
1. Kansas City Chiefs (Football team)–History. 2. Arrowhead
Stadium (Kansas City, Mo.)–History. I. Title.
GV956.K35M35 1997
796.332'64'0977844—dc21   97-13388
CIP

Acknowledgments

Many, many persons made this project come to life with their knowledge and recollections, and not all of them made it into the text. But each will know his or her contribution, and the author is eternally grateful for every nugget that enhances the work. First and foremost, a hardy round of applause for every individual in the Chiefs family who works to make Arrowhead Stadium a pleasurable and entertaining place to attend events, and who makes us feel welcome and comfortable every time we enter.

Public Relations Director Bob Moore and his tireless staff provided invaluable resources with great patience, God love 'em. As if they aren't busy enough: assistant director Jim Carr, assistant Pete Moris, community relations manager Brenda Sniezek, and administrative assistant Eileen Weir.

And to the people who keep them hopping—the sports reporters of newspaper, radio and television who gave unselfishly of their recall (especially dear friends Joe McGuff, Bill "Dad" Richardson, Jon Rand, Kent Pulliam, and Randy Covitz from *Star* days)—your stories and historical perspectives were wonderful. Managing Editor Greg Echlin, a friend in radio, provided rich research. Bob Sprenger, former Chiefs PR director, was a treasure chest.

Further, on the Chiefs' staff, thanks to: Anita McDonald, Gary Spani, Donna Scott, Sheldon Mickey, Dan Mears, and K.C. Wolf in sales and marketing; the persons who have headed that department—Russ Kline, Phil Thomas, and Wallace Bennett; the director of ticket operations, Doug Hopkins, and his staff; the director of development, Ken Blume, and his staff; and the director of stadium operations, Jeff Klein, and his staff.

Lynn Stiles, Terry Bradway and Mark Hatley opened the player personnel department for insights and memories of player procurement. Head trainer Dave Kendall and equipment manager Mike Davidson made us feel at home in their clubhouse quarters, and equipment assistant Allen Wright showed us how to paint nose bandages!

Obviously, the cooperation of Dennis Watley, the Vice President of Administration, and the entire administrative group in Carl Peterson's wing provided immeasurable support. A special mention goes to executive secretaries Barbara Harrington, who retired from Peterson's office, Carol Modean in Watley's sector, and Nadine Steffan in the office of assistant general manager Denny Thum. They found the big guys when we needed them, rode herd on corrected text, and smiled all the while.

And there is no way this work would have come together without the abilities of Judy Tewksbury, who coordinates the Hunt Sports office of Jack Steadman and Tim Connolly, and dear, dear Susie Napoli in Dallas, the executive assistant to Lamar Hunt, who deciphered his notations and kept us in touch. However does she keep up with him?

A note of memory is a must: Jean Finn, who died Aug. 1, 1997. She was a Hunt family personal secretary for 36 years into her 70s.

Retired architect Ralph Myers and his wife Sharon opened their home and history books to us, arranged by Mary Axetell, a VP at HNTB. Ron Labinski at HOK Sports had a wealth of first-hand knowledge, his executive assistant Rose Howland coordinated it, and his wife Lee introduced us to many good people and sources.

Two people deserve mention for keeping names straight: Jan Stenerud, both in Chiefs and stadium history, and Janie Lewis, who rules over the door to the Gold Suite.

The family at Addax Publishing Group deserves a trophy for endurance, patience, tolerance, kindness, and—especially—professionalism in making this total team effort come together. Personal thanks to Bob and Sharon Snodgrass, Darcie Kidson, Brad Breon, David Power, and Michelle Washington for every effort that held the project intact.

Table of Contents

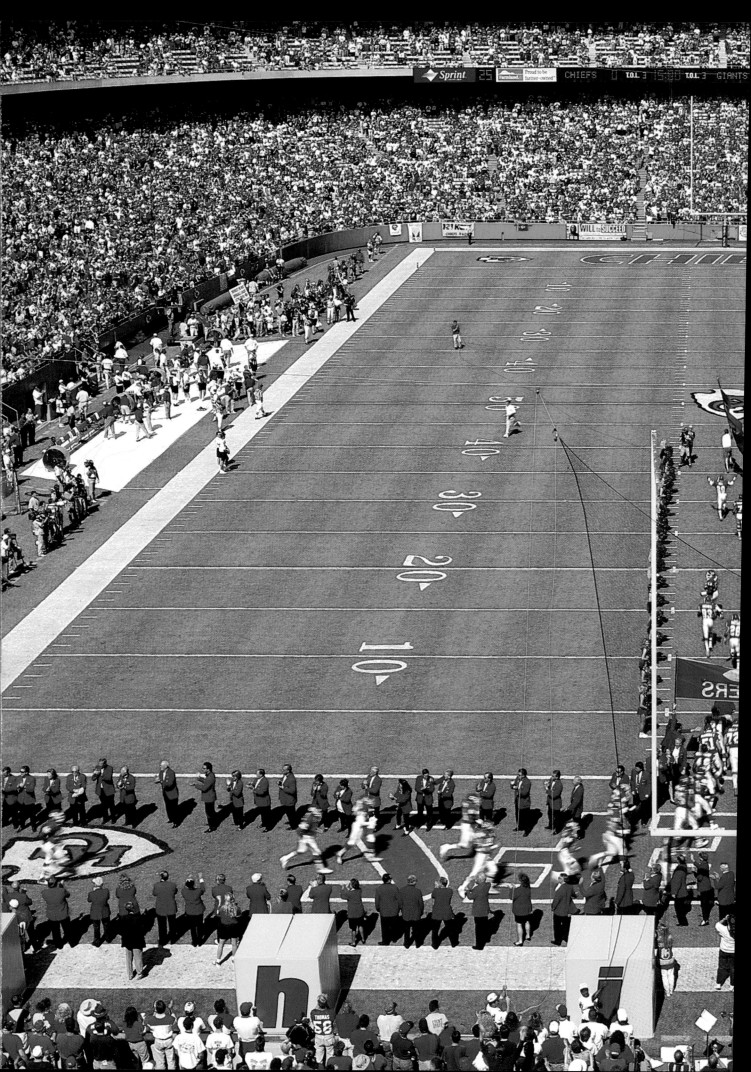

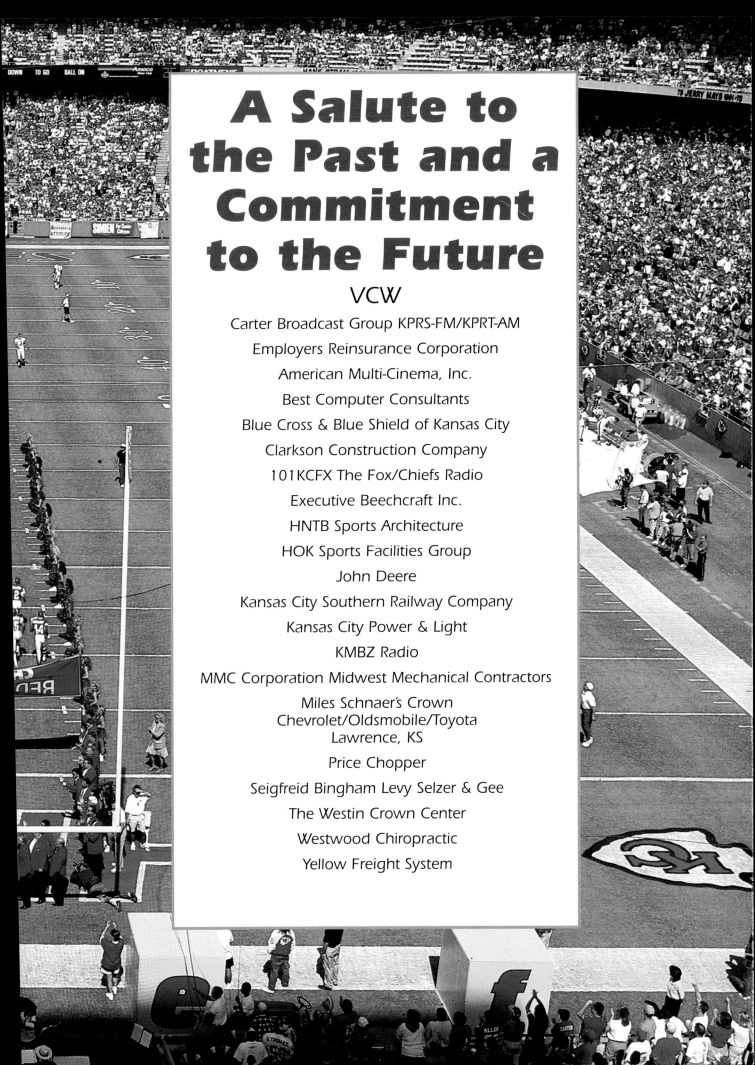

A Salute to the Past and a Commitment to the Future

VCW

Carter Broadcast Group KPRS-FM/KPRT-AM

Employers Reinsurance Corporation

American Multi-Cinema, Inc.

Best Computer Consultants

Blue Cross & Blue Shield of Kansas City

Clarkson Construction Company

101KCFX The Fox/Chiefs Radio

Executive Beechcraft Inc.

HNTB Sports Architecture

HOK Sports Facilities Group

John Deere

Kansas City Southern Railway Company

Kansas City Power & Light

KMBZ Radio

MMC Corporation Midwest Mechanical Contractors

Miles Schnaer's Crown
Chevrolet/Oldsmobile/Toyota
Lawrence, KS

Price Chopper

Seigfreid Bingham Levy Selzer & Gee

The Westin Crown Center

Westwood Chiropractic

Yellow Freight System

Foreword
by Lamar Hunt

WHENEVER I PAUSE TO REMINISCE ABOUT THE QUARTER OF A CENTURY that has flown by since Arrowhead Stadium opened, seemingly at the speed of the military flyovers that have been a highlight of many game days, a variety of thoughts pass through my mind.

Thoughts of the wrangling that took place to create and construct Arrowhead and the magnificent Truman Sports Complex. Thoughts of the pageantry of opening night and - we can laugh about it now - the struggle right up to the 11th hour to stage the inaugural game - the 1972 Governor's Cup showdown against the St. Louis Cardinals - overcoming considerable odds after two major construction shutdowns.

Thoughts, certainly, of all the outstanding players, coaches and Chiefs management personnel from the floor of the field to the highest photo position above. The personalities, after all, are what bring life and a sense of history to any public arena and we have been blessed with dedicated and diligent staff, outstanding management and scores of brilliant, on-field performers who have added luster to one of the finest architectural settings in all of sports.

The memory bank is full with admiration for those who have given life to and cared for Arrowhead, but one group keeps stepping to the fore: the Chiefs fans. Arrowhead stands as a monument to the loyalty, energy, and fervor of our fans. One of the highlights of game day for me is a walk through the parking lots and around the tailgate tent areas. I love seeing the race for prime tailgate positions, the variety of flags on taller and taller poles, hearing the music, absorbing the aroma from the thousands of pre-

Arrowhead ice sculpture to kick off 25th anniversary celebration.

feasts, and watching the red swarm pressing toward the stadium - all caught up in Chiefs fever and ready for some football.

The Chiefs organization will continue to put forth a maximum effort to reward that loyalty with the best possible game day experience. As time marches on, we can be proud of the foresight and creativity that made Arrowhead a futuristic milestone in stadium design which continues to draw rave architectural reviews on its 25th birthday.

For all of these memories, I express a heartfelt, "Thank You", as we stroll through the pictorial history along the perimeter of all the good times had at *Arrowhead: Home of the Chiefs*.

Sincerely,

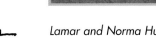

Lamar Hunt
Founder

Lamar and Norma Hunt (photo by Tom Mitchell)

Prelude to the Story of Arrowhead

T O CAPTURE THE FULL FLAVOR OF THE birth of Arrowhead Stadium, let's delve much further back than 25 years–all the way to a time when Kansas City had no professional football team, but had an insightful and visionary mayor, for whom, by the way, the Chiefs are named.

H. Roe Bartle, popularly known as "The Chief," sat in the Mayor's chair during the early 1960s. And one Sunday while watching a football game on television, one of those light bulbs came on over his head.

Make note of that Sunday: Dec. 23, 1962. Bartle was watching the championship game of the upstart, three-year-old American Football League featuring the Dallas Texans and the Houston Oilers, an event that came to be known as "Football's Longest Day." In Kansas City sports history, it can now be viewed also as "The Fateful Day"–the day of conception for both the Chiefs and, much later, Arrowhead Stadium.

Jack Steadman, Lamar Hunt's top financial aide and the unofficial historian for his early years in pro football, recalled, "Lamar got a call the next day (after the game) from a man who said he was the mayor of Kansas City, wanting to know if he would consider moving his football team to Mid-America."

Thus, with vision and boldness Roe Bartle and Lamar Hunt sewed, fertilized and grew the seeds of Chiefs football, and Arrowhead Stadium was among the many rewards reaped from the venture.

The finished product arose after several years of planning, plotting, and political harangue. The concept for Arrowhead (and the entire Harry S. Truman Sports Complex) ran a gamut, and a gauntlet, of ideas from a domed stadium and observation tower like Seattle's Space Needle, to a rolling roof over separate baseball and football stadiums in the center of a theme park. All through the development of Arrowhead's location and architectural style, Hunt had but one requirement: "It had to have at least 75,001 seats," he said, smiling mischievously. "Know why I had a bee in my bonnet?

The Cotton Bowl had 75,000."

That was the Texans/Chiefs' previous home in Dallas. Some football-minded folks in Dallas, thinking Hunt a nut along the order of, say, an Edison or Bell with his AFL invention, suggested that he not utilize a stadium the size of the Cotton Bowl–which was the only choice in Dallas at the time. Avoid playing to partially-full seating, went their conventional wisdom … which ultimately proved short-sighted.

That notion was based on Hunt's Texans and their NFL competitors, the Cowboys, drawing scant attendance during the three-season period of 1960–'62-an average of scarcely 10,000 paid for each team. "Clearly, it was not a two-team market," Hunt said.

Thirty-odd years later Hunt proudly displayed the attendance records that show at least one crowd of 70,000-plus in all but three seasons at Arrowhead (two of which were strike years of disenchantment and alienation among NFL fans). Starting in 1994, the Chiefs led the NFL in home attendance three consecutive seasons, including the 1996 25th anniversary year, and showed no signs of letting go of that grip after 99.4 percent of season ticket holders renewed for 1997 while a long, long waiting list grew longer.

Following the weave through the patterns of Arrowhead history, the threads criss-cross in many directions, forming designs borne of innumerable minds and spirits, offices, drawing boards, boardrooms, rumors, strikes, backhoes, backbone, schmoozing and gumption. The dream weavers range from architects to engineers, politicos to CEOs, earth movers to movers and shakers, and taxpayers seeing red to ticket sellers in red coats to red-clad ticket buyers in red seats.

For fear of leaving somebody out, the focus of this body of work will narrow to the man whose derring do created the Chiefs, Lamar Hunt; his top general in charge of organizing and rallying the troops, Jack Steadman; and three collective bodies without whom Arrowhead (and the Chiefs, for that matter) would never have entered the collective mind of Kansas City:

- The football team, with its inordinate success under the guiding hand of its inventive, masterful coach, Hank Stram;

- The Chiefs Club of civic boosters, which included the super-seller Red Coaters who met the requirement of selling 100 or more season tickets to earn their special blazer;

- The civic leaders, legislators and taxpayers of Kansas City and Jackson County.

The Chiefs Club sales group sprang from a conversation among Hunt, Steadman and Bartle when the Texans braintrust met secretly with the Kansas City mayor. Bartle, after watching that fateful AFL playoff game, called Hunt and said he understood that because the two startup teams in Dallas were suffering small crowds, the Texans might be searching for a place to move.

Steadman, the club's general manager, said that they had not, at that point, considered anything specific about a move, although they had held serious discussions about the options or opportunities that must be considered if the Texans were to become a viable contributor to the AFL. With that mindset, he and Hunt figured that a visit with Kansas City's mayor might stimulate some possibilities, at least moving them off center to plot the future of the club.

"Lamar and I quietly came to Kansas City," Steadman recalled. "We were headed to the NCAA convention in Los Angeles anyway, so it was sort of on the way. When we got there, we encountered the most unforgettable character we'd ever met."

During their session Bartle asked what it would take to get the Texans to pull up stakes and become Kansas City's team. Hunt and Steadman put their heads together, juggled a few numbers, and decided that 25,000 season tickets would would be a proper minimum requirement. (Later, an analysis showed 15,000 as a break-even point.)

Bartle punched up a call on speakerphone to the president of the Kansas City Chamber of Commerce, Bill Dauer, and said simply, "I have some gentlemen in my office representing a professional football team. If we could bring this team to town, could we sell 25,000 season tickets?" After a pause, a voice rang through the speakerphone, "We'll get it done."

From those simple, direct and quick conversations, a five-year deal was formulated, to be sealed later—one selling point of which was the enticing $1 a year rent. Things progressed under a cloak of some secrecy. During the early negotiations

Hunt, who had just turned 30, was called "Mr. Lamar." And Steadman was known as "Jack X."

The Chiefs Club formed around sports booster supreme Ray Evans, a former All-America in both football and basketball at the University of Kansas, and, at that time, head of Trader's National Bank.

The club members went forth into the community and sold thousands upon thousands of season tickets to buyers on the simple approach that Kansas City had a chance to obtain a pro football team and it required their support. Most of the ticket sellers didn't know what team or what league, relatively few knew much about the AFL or its quality of play. Fans of football, and fans of progress, just got out their checkbooks and wrote history. It bowled over Hunt and Steadman.

Steadman moved to town and operated anonymously for a while. He enjoyed a good laugh over the recollection of Bartle introducing him to people. "He'd say, 'He is an IRS agent in town investigating the expense accounts of some of our most prominent citizens." In those early days of 1963 Steadman worked on the location of the practice facility and offices with virtually no one knowing what organization he represented.

Two key people knew what was up. Herb Hoffman was the city attorney and he worked on agreements covering a stadium lease and the building of practice facilities and offices for the team. Jerry Cohen was the commissioner of parks, appointed by the mayor, and he had to obtain approval from the parks board of directors. And then, in mid-February, a public announcement was forthcoming from Lamar Hunt of an intent to move the Texans to town, contingent on season ticket sales.

Complications set in. Some stemmed from Bartle making promises in January, and then getting displaced by attorney Ike Davis in the April mayoral election. Another was that by May, when a final decision by Hunt was imminent, about 14,000 tickets were sold–almost to, but short of the all-important break-even point. "We decided, 'Let's do it!' We agreed to everything with nothing in writing, packed up and moved," Steadman said. By the time the season started, season ticket sales stood at an AFL record 15,123.

Kansas City had turned a corner for the new league. And the stage was set for a new stadium, although there were many obstacles still to overcome.

The team had to start in storied, but old and dilapidated Municipal Stadium, sharing it with the woeful Athletics of baseball's American League. "The early years were difficult," Hunt said. The team struggled through losing records the first two seasons, and by 1965 season ticket sales had eroded to 9,182. Then three things happened that turned the tide: a winning season, an emotional bonding through a tragedy, and a civic season-ticket campaign. The Wolfpack ticket-selling project was already planned as the '65 season wound down.

And, just before the Chiefs concluded their 7-5-2 season, budding young star running back Mack Lee Hill died during surgery on his knee. "This wasn't a player who came from Dallas, he was Kansas City's own young future star," Hunt said. "Suddenly, he was gone. You could sense that it created a community feeling for the team that hadn't existed before."

By April of the off-season, the turnaround boost in season tickets surpassed the goal of 20,000, and eventually reached 22,000. Then, two more catalysts occurred in 1966–merger and championship. The pro football merger of the NFL and AFL, and the Chiefs' championship play that culminated in an appearance in the first Super Bowl created a groundswell movement toward building a new stadium.

Interest and excitement rose to unimagined peaks. Search parties traversed far and wide to find land and funding and, consequently, to locate voters favoring a new football home for the Chiefs. Hunt refers to the resultant project as "a melding of architectural genius, proper financial planning, volunteer spirit and community commitment."

Specifics in the assembly of minds, monies and matters leading up to the creation of Arrowhead at the Truman Sports Complex will delight you, as certainly the players on the stage will, too. Five Pro Football Hall of Fame players carried over into Arrowhead Stadium's early years from the Super Bowl glory days under Stram, as well as a long parade of other players bearing various degrees of talent and personality. Others were bound for the Hall after they passed through Arrowhead, adding to its glitter. Certainly without the Chiefs' relatively quick successes in Kansas City, a stadium project would have been a far larger obstacle to clear.

By book's end you will have sensed the spirit that Arrowhead inspired for the developers, for the people who have played and worked there, and for the legions of football faithful who have packed the house, through gloriously thick and sometimes agonizingly thin eras, and helped make Arrowhead more than just a tribute to creative architecture.

The home of the Chiefs is, yes, a magnificent entertainment facility, but without its people it is nothing more than just another pretty hunk of concrete imposed on the skyline. Beyond its aesthetic splendor, Arrowhead is its occupants, its masses–the people on the field and in the stands WHO WILL, WHO WILL ROCK YOU ...

"From the moment you drive into the complex until you leave, someone is there to help you have an enjoyable experience. We have security people patrol on carts. The extra amenities-like charcoal disposal units for the tailgaters, to keep the cooking from being illegal because of the safety factor, and concessions and portable toilets outside before the gates open. We have the fifth-largest parking lot in the NFL, and it's jammed. Inside, the sight lines are magnificent, and the atmosphere generated is like a college crowd the way they all cheer in concert. Chiefs Sundays are definitely a significant family event, including women and children."

Bob Moore, Director of Public Relations

Chapter 1
History of Arrowhead: From Dallas to Today

WHEN THE HISTORY OF ARROWHEAD STADIUM becomes a point of discussion, one name crops up more than any other. From Chiefs owner Lamar Hunt through a cadre of architects, designers, engineers and construction kingpins, all angles flow back to Jack Steadman's desk. He has ridden shotgun over Hunt's financial affairs since Hunt was a baby in business, ascending to the head chair on the board that governs the Chiefs and the Hunt Midwest Enterprises empire of mining and real estate development.

Jack Steadman (© Young Company)

Although several minds and hands brought Arrowhead Stadium to fruition, the Chiefs media guide states in no uncertain terms, "Steadman conceived the idea of Kansas City building the dual Harry S. Truman Sports complex…" And whoever might want to put a different spin on it, no individual knows more about that situation, from conception through incubation to the pounding of the final nail and the turning of the first turnstile.

It is a coincidence of the highest order that "stead" is the root word in steady, steadfast, and Steadman. He guided the notion of a beyond-modern facility through volatile and turbulent political and community unrest, melding the striking egos, striking personalities, striking unions, until the steepled four corners of Arrowhead struck the Jackson County horizon and became a salute to all that is good about autumn and winter Sundays in the National Football League.

"Make no mistake, this was Jack Steadman's baby," said Joe McGuff, who reported on the entire Arrowhead process for the Kansas City Star and years later became president of the Greater Kansas City Sports Commission. "He set up shop out there and literally pushed them into that 1972 opening."

Steadman obliged to provide the timeline, the nuances of circumstance that traces the origination of Arrowhead in its 25th year of splendid existence.

We know how the ambition of the mayor, "Chief" Roe Bartle, rattled the political chains until the noise reached a crescendo the public couldn't ignore. We know of Lamar Hunt's youthful zest and dream-thinking. Without either, we have no Chiefs, we have no Truman Complex, we have no story.

But many other players romped across this field of schemes before the bond issue passed. Some are obvious-the conceivers and contructors, the public officials and the voters. Some remain in the background, to mingle in the cast of thousands. Some unusual circumstances make good storytelling among them, especially one famous and infamous

Construction crew at Arrowhead.

"We definitely had formed a Mutual Degradation Society," Steadman said, only half laughing, but still nettled 31 years later by how obnoxious one man could be, especially over a venture that held so much potential good fortune for everyone-owners, and community.

man whose mule cast the city in unwanted light.

Oddly, for example, the owner of Kansas City's major league baseball team in the '60s, the inimitable, irrascible, impossible Charles O. Finley, had some bearing on the underpinnings of new stadia. He was the tenant at Municipal Stadium when the Chiefs came to town in 1963, and he yelped that he wasn't consulted when the city gave the Chiefs a $1 a year rental fee and made improvements at the old ballpark to accommodate football. The city spent about $700,000 on amenities, mostly press box renovation and installation of bleacher seats (where the renowned "Wolfpack" of rabid fans formed).

The two teams had to coexist. Steadman met repeatedly with Finley and his right hand, general manager Pat Friday, to determine how operating procedures and costs would work, such as groundkeeper George Toma's time. "I'd no sooner get out of the room and they'd change the deal," Steadman said. "It was to the point he (Finley) was about to drive me nuts."

Eventually, Finley's rantings and threats to move the team, his constant uncooperative behavior, and, what was worse for Steadman, letting Hunt's staff handle all the work with Kansas City's politicos-all of that pushed the desire and talk about a new facility away from a multipurpose, two-sport stadium. Possibly those initial creative processes might have come around to a dual-stadium concept anyway, but certainly the disinterest and belligerence of Charlie O. did much to push Hunt, Steadman & Cohorts in that direction.

The genesis of stadium talk, amid Finley's loud noises about build-one-or-else-I'm-outta-here and Hunt/Steadman's need to solidify the franchise's future through expansion, arose from the availability of $43 million of funds designated for a stadium from Jackson County's $102 million bonding capacity. The city worked hand in glove with the county in utilizing those funds.

Heavyweights lined up to support the effort. And factions formed, in business, in government, all around the town. But, overall, a positiveness prevailed in the air. The expressed need for Kansas City to shed, or at least modify, its cowtown image fueled the longing for another professional sport, specifically football, and ultimately, special interests and egos aside, the public's will was the way.

The Chiefs Club had formed, following the lead of banker and sports enthusiast Ray Evans, who served as its president for 15 years, and, amazingly, that band of citizens sold thousands of season tickets to lure a pro football team to town without anybody knowing which team or which league, or even whether there really would be a team in Kansas City. Community support was astounding in expressing desire and faith.

May Day! May Day! A distress call? To the contrary. That was the date in 1963-May 1-that the announcement was forthcoming: the Dallas Texans, champions of the American Football League, were relocating in Kansas City, to become known as the Chiefs. A board of directors formed across community lines. By the next year talk heated up over the stadium issue.

Several men moved to the fore of the project-new mayor Ike Davis; the Kansas City Chamber of Commerce; Jackson County judges Morris Dubiner, Charles Curry, Charles Wheeler, Alex Petrovic, George Lear; the non-partisan Jackson County Sports Authority appointed by Gov. Warren Hearnes; the Greater Kansas City Sports Commission; assorted businessmen like Leon Brownfield and Ray Evans and Harry Darby; design architect Charles Deaton and the architectural firm of Kivett and Myers, led by partner Ralph Myers, Truman Complex project manager Bill Love, his assistant Bill Wunsch, and Arrowhead project architect Ron Labinski; general contractors Phil Sharp and his son, Don, in an alliance with contractors Del Webb and Walter Kidde.

Even now, as then, it is a sticky wicket to single out individuals, for fear of wounding an ego or understating a role, as dozens upon hundreds eventually became involved in important and unique ways, from the brainstorm through the maelstrom of political and construction activity. Summarily, Bill Clarkson, one of the Sports Authority appointees who became its president and served nine years, said that "...you cannot credit Lamar Hunt enough . . . but the genesis of my thoughts about the project is Morris Dubiner."

Among the move-and-shake crowd, Dubiner became the singlemost influential, wielding the most clout on the stadium pitch. He was elected to the Jackson County court, presiding over the Eastern sector. Openly known as an avid sports fan who championed the value of professional franchises to the community, he stirred interest in a new bond proposal late in 1964 with the

Inside Arrowhead construction.

words "all-sports stadium" written all over it. Sadly, he died a year before the stadium opened.

Dubiner had whispered in the ear of prominent KC civic and business linchpin Dutton Brookfield, founder of Unitog, to further the cause of getting the stadium into the bond package.

The other judges of Jackson County, Charles Curry and Charles Wheeler, became entwined in the issue as it gained steam and favor (and later Petrovic, who replaced Dubiner). They joined forces with a citizens group spurred by Evans and his father-in-law, Darby, and the sports editor of *The Kansas City Star,* Ernie Mehl, and by the spring of '65 the bond proposal was a reality.

Because of strong political overtones, mostly emanating from Dubiner's push and shove, the state set up a neutral body to oversee the whole matter. "Morris also had the ear of the governor for appointments," Clarkson said. "He lobbied in Jefferson City, where Kansas Citian William Morris was lieutenant governor, and Morris recommended the forming of the Authority."

The original Sports Authority comprised Brookfield as the chair, Clarkson (who was in the construction business), Bishop G. Leslie DeLapp ("the honesty factor," Steadman said, smiling in reference to DeLapp's association with the Latter Day Saints in Independence, Mo.), businessman Harry Moreland, and the president of the local Teamsters, Karl "Curly" Rogers. "When they were appointed, the ball got rolling with us (Hunt) and Finley," Steadman said.

Clarkson said, "The Authority gave some basis for credibility for creation of a stadium."

Finley, however, continued to whine and threaten, and the ominous shroud he cast over the existence of the A's-"Build me a new stadium...I'm leaving...I'll stay, probably, but, maybe..." - steered thoughts away from an all-sports stadium. He drove a wedge between himself and not only the public, but Hunt and Steadman. "He hurt the psyce of the whole city, always talking about how bad it was," Hunt said.

Brookfield and the politicians made it clear that if a new stadium materialized, its tenants would be responsible for all maintenance and operating costs. "Finley was never interested in our stadium proposals, always saying he was upset and going to move," Steadman said. "I was showing a lot of interest and working it, and ultimately we were staffing his work for the Sports Authority, too, behind the scenes. Aside from making me crazy, he made us realize that we didn't want to be co-dependent on a team that might leave, which, of course, happened before the stadium was built."

Foresight kicked in. Studies showed that a dome would cost at least $130 million, and Kansas City had $43 million to work with. Again, the threat of winding up in it alone was enough to make the football faction shudder. "We'd be stuck operating it," Steadman said.

No multipurpose stadium, let alone a massive dome, was feasible for an organization that would use it essentially just 12 games a year in a five-month season; without a baseball team sharing the load, well, you do the math. So, even the less costly two-sport, open-air arenas that were springing up everywhere held no appeal.

Also, and even more of a factor, the Chiefs, with championship caliber drawing power, already were averaging crowds of 42,000. With their growth potential, it wouldn't fit in a 50,000-or-so stadium. "We believed strongly that the great franchises of the future would have big stadiums," Steadman said, which, we know, was prescient. By the time Arrowhead opened, 72,000 seats were sold in advance.

Further, the two sports were incompatible for sight lines. To accommodate a diamond, football loses valuable close-up sideline seats. During the first weeks of 1966 Steadman called Brookfield and said, "Dutton, we don't want to be tied to baseball. What we need is a new football stadium

somewhere." Soon thereafter, talks shifted to dual stadiums, and a sliding dome, a futuristic folly that tickled the fancy of the folks who would have to vote this whole thing in-the Charles Deaton story. It eventually fell through because of costs.

The site became another burning issue. First, it was to be a plot north of downtown along the Missouri river bank, owned by the city, the place which has since become a nation of impounded cars. Next, attention turned to directly across south from Bartle Hall, undeveloped at the time where a throughway was planned to run alongside. Then, the downtown airport. By the time the stadium was voted on, 18 sites had been examined and mostly rejected.

Clarkson said, "The biggest knock on downtown was that it had only 500 owners of real estate. A big perplexing problem was parking, especially if we had a dome. It would cost $2,500 a space, rivaling the cost of the stadium. And frankly, what convinced us not to go downtown was the Chiefs' decision to have their own stadium. Two stadiums downtown? No way."

One day Brookfield got a call about a privately-owned plot of 500 acres that the family would let go at $5,000 an acre. Steadman went with him to assess it. Steadman recalled, "It was almost as if God had dropped this in our lap." It afforded ample space for parking and two stadia. Brookfield informed the Jackson County judges, who in turn said, "We'll buy the property." The county and state built the off-roadway ramp system and widened Blue Ridge Cutoff, with federal funding support. That saved all of the bond money for the facilities-a twin stadium complex, upward to 80,000 for football and 40,000-plus for baseball, with parking in between and all around.

Bill Love, a senior partner in Kivett and Myers, said in retrospect, "The site was very unusual, almost a natural valley that fit both stadiums so perfectly. It was almost as if the site was predestined for the sports complex."

A sequence of events started in 1965 that solidified the project. In short, complete Kansas City football madness set in. Its team was good, even though it didn't land its sensational No. 1 draft pick, running back phenom Gale Sayers of Kansas, who opted for the Chicago Bears in the traditional league. Still, the AFL was gaining respect and credibility. The upstart "other" league turned heads by declaring war when the NFL made its first raid on talent, signing placekicker Pete Gogolak away from the Buffalo Bills to the New York Giants. The AFL appointed Al Davis as commissioner and he planned a rebel effort in an attempt to lure NFL stars-the drawing power for a pro football franchise.

Common sense led to Hunts conversations in April of '66 with Tex Schramm, then president of the Cowboys, and the two leagues agreed to merge. The Chiefs had just scored large when Heisman Trophy winner Mike Garrett chose them over his hometown Los Angeles Rams. Joe Namath had signed in 1965 with the Jets and these successes brought the NFL to its knees. When they merged, the Chiefs Club with its Red Coaters (those who sold 100 or more season tickets) gained momentum.

A few months later the Chiefs added one more selling point for tickets, stadium, and a lifelong love affair-the quintessential selling point-by appearing in the first AFL-NFL championship showdown in January 1967 (a game which later became known as the first Super Bowl). Even though the Chiefs lost to Green Bay, the game was a godsend to the Chiefs Club in its ticket drive, as fervor for the team ran way off the chart.

Steadman said, "We didn't win (Super Bowl I), but we came home to the biggest Chiefs fever ever. It was crazy. Vince Lombardi had set the table when he criticized our league, saying something like, 'They (AFL) are okay, but they are not at our level.' It caused a furious outpouring from fans. From the unfinished TWA runway at KCI all the way into town, people in cars were yelling and cheering. I called Dutton Brookfield the next day and said, 'Dutton, we've got to go forward on this. How fast can we get it before the public?' We kept fanning the momentum, and got it together by June 23, 1967 (voting day for the bond issue)."

At the heart of that support was that group known fondly (and not so fondly by opponents) as "The Wolfpack" who sat in specially-built bleachers added onto old Municipal Stadium for football, upward to 7,000 strong. The majority of them formed the nucleus of carryover season ticket holders when Arrowhead started selling out.

Thank one more entity for Arrowhead: baseball's American League. Under pressure from Missouri senator Stuart Symington's lobby to kill the antitrust exemption, buffered by a civic push from

the newly-formed Sports Commission with Earl Smith driving it and from sports editor Ernie Mehl and *Kansas City Star* endorsements, the AL awarded Kansas City a new franchise to start in 1968, leaving only a one-year gap.

"That was very much a part of passing the bond election," Steadman said. The necessary vote seemed at the time "virtually impossible," he recalled. "Unfortunately, public polls showed that all parts of the $102 million bond would pass except the stadium portion. You could vote on each phase of the bond separately."

A two-thirds majority was required. Three weeks before the election polls showed 60 percent favoring. Dutton Brookfield told Steadman, "Jack, it's dead." Enter, again, the Chiefs Club. With a concerted effort to get voters to the booth, the backers-about 100 of them in red coats-passed out flyers, gave rides, everything possible, and the bond passed with 68.1 percent in favor. The Chiefs got a boost from government officials, too; Lt. Gov. Morris lent his clout to rallying the voters behind the stadium.

"We had everything going right," Steadman summarized, "and we took advantage of the timing. Dutton was so good at generating community support. We got endorsements from all the factions."

At the celebration of the Chiefs' 25th year in Arrowhead, Petrovic commented, "Lamar had created a spark. We had to strike while the iron was hot."

From there, down hill coasting, right? Or, as Steadman put it, "Now you think you're home free." Groundbreaking occurred in 1968. Joe Tobin underbid by $1 million and spent a year moving 5 million yards of earth and rock to create bowls. "He's an earth-moving legend," Clarkson said. "His crews just kept pecking away, and watching from I-70 they looked like little kiddie cars down there hauling dirt away."

Dirt had scarcely been moved, though, when union business wreaked havoc. Strike one. The Chiefs negotiated, meanwhile, for stadium operations contracts. "We wanted to control our own destiny, not have the county and city control it," Steadman said.

Brookfield had proposed another $1 deal. "It never had a prayer," Steadman said. Judge Curry opposed vehemently, under the guise of supporting local business interests, such as a proposed

Lamar Hunt and the AFL

I N THE FRONT LOBBY OF THE CHIEFS' practice facility located prominently at the Truman Sports Complex, a display of photos and documents details the history of the Chiefs. One cluster of memorabilia features several pages of stationary bearing an American Airlines logo and containing handwritten notes. Lamar Hunt wrote them.

In 1959 Hunt took rapid and stunning action on those notes that helped reshape the world of professional football. Without those decisive steps, perhaps there never would have been a Texans/Chiefs football team, nor an Arrowhead Stadium, nor anything else associated with the various Hunt enterprises in the Kansas City area.

Hunt scribbled the notes during a flight home from a meeting at which he had hoped to buy into a team in the National Football League. He met with rejection because he wanted to move the team, the Chicago Cardinals, to Dallas. He had been on a year-long quest for an NFL team to relocate to his home town. The Cardinals, on Chicago's south side playing in Comiskey Park, needed operating capital as they were locked into a bitter rivalry for fans against the northside Chicago Bears. Hunt recalled, "They were death enemies."

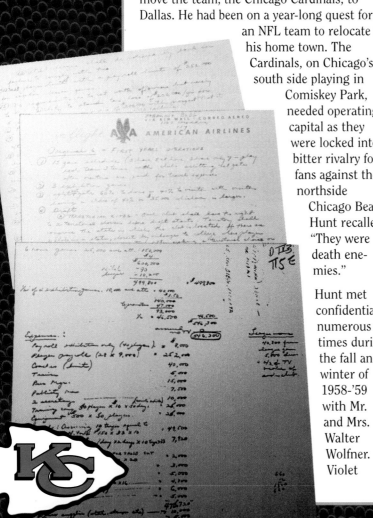

Hunt met confidentially numerous times during the fall and winter of 1958-'59 with Mr. and Mrs. Walter Wolfner. Violet

Wolfner was the widow of Cardinals founder Charles Bidwell, and her second husband, Walter, was the club's general manager. "... Various names would creep into our conversations," Hunt said. "For example, one time she asked me, 'Do you know a man named Bud Adams in Houston?' I told her no, and she said, 'Well, he wants the Cardinals, too.'"

Before long Hunt had a miniature prospect list of numerous persons interested in acquiring the Cardinals for their respective cities, among them Adams, Max Winter in Minneapolis, Bob Howsam in Denver, and others in different locales.

After one final meeting with the Wolfners at their winter home in Florida, Hunt made the long, historic flight home from Miami early in 1959. He had offered to purchase 30 percent of their team. The Wolfners were willing to partner with him, because of their financial needs, but they were not willing to move to Dallas… at least not right away. As Hunt recalled, their response was, "Join us in the Chicago ownership, and maybe someday in the future we will look at Dallas."

So Hunt's mind started working overtime as he returned to Dallas. "I can still see that plane," he said 38 years later during the 25th anniversary year of Arrowhead. "It was a commercial prop flight, and I was in the front, right-hand seat. It was like the proverbial light bulb came on over my head. It was obvious the NFL was not going to expand. So I thought: 'a new league.' I wondered what would happen if I sought out all those people who had expressed interest in the Cardinals. Baseball had two leagues. Why wouldn't a second league work in football?"

Voila! The moment of conception of the American Football League. Hunt said in reflection, "It's literally the only time I can recall such a defining moment where an idea immediately became a reality for me." Hunt, just 26 at the time, promptly turned his attention to locating the possible team owners, none of whom he knew.

He scored on Bud Adams and Houston right away. Adams loved the notion. "Two big plums—a Dallas-Houston rivalry, us in the

Cotton Bowl, them in Rice Stadium. It was perfect," Hunt said. Four other individual meetings followed in rapid succession, and eventually he set up the first group meeting on Aug. 15, 1959 at which the formal organization of the new league took place.

"I was the common thread, but none of the prospective American Football League owners had ever met one another until that important initial gathering in Chicago," Hunt said. "There were no letters of intent or handshakes prior to the meeting, but all had told me they would come." The group comprised Hunt, Adams, Howsam, Winter and his two partners, Bill Boyer and H.P. Skoglund, Harry Wismer representing New York City, and Barron Hilton speaking for Los Angeles.

The AFL was set to go with six charter members–Dallas, Houston, Denver, Minneapolis, New York, and Los Angeles. Each agreed to place $25,000 in the league treasury, and the owners signed formal papers in Dallas on Aug. 22.

Meanwhile, Ralph Wilson read about the new league in the press and he contacted Hunt by letter. Wilson, who was from Detroit, wanted to place a team in Miami, but couldn't nail down a deal with the Orange Bowl, so he located his team in Buffalo. And finally, Billy Sullivan expressed an interest; Hunt contacted him by phone, gave Sullivan a deadline of a few days to come up with the $25,000 franchise fee, and Boston entered the fold. Later that fall, after the league's first-ever player draft, Winter withdrew and instead committed Minneapolis to the NFL as an expansion team.

The group searched to replace Minneapolis and found Wayne Valley. In late January 1960 Valley and seven others from the San Francisco Bay area founded the Oakland Raiders, thus completing the AFL's first complement of teams.

Years later, Hunt pointed out that those original notes scratched on the airline stationery contained items such as a hypothetical budget of what it would take to make a team work–such as 15,000 fans a game buying $4 tickets for seven home games, "… that sort of thing, just to see if it would fly," he said.

Those were naive times, but take a look at it now …

Voting Day on the Bond Issue

THE SPUNK, THE DEPTH OF COMMITMENT, the flaming desire, and the tenacious determination of the sports-driven, civic-minded backers of the Truman Sports Complex never surfaced any more amazingly as on voting day on the bond issue, June 1967.

This wasn't a project that needed a simple majority by the voters to pass. A two-thirds majority was needed! A vote "yes" would approve the $43 million allocated for a stadium in Jackson County, and voters could vote on every portion of the total $102 million bond issue (other parts were designated for streets, schools, etc.). The sports complex had to pass on its own merit. The requirement seemed out of reach. Polls showed that all parts of the bond issue would pass except the stadium portion. It was a very long shot at best, and virtually impossible in the minds of its backers.

About three weeks before the election, the core group working behind the scenes on attaining the two-stadium deal learned that about 60 percent of the constituents favored it, and that wouldn't pass. Dutton Brookfield

called Jack Steadman and said, "Jack, it's dead."

The Chiefs Club board of directors convened quickly. Dick Docking recommended a colleague who was well-versed in setting up a telephone campaign to get voters to turn out; he had helped Docking's brother, Bob, in his election to the governorship of Kansas. Ray Evans, Chiefs Club president, set up a phone bank in his office at Traders National Bank.

Chiefs Club members called every block in every ward in every precinct to find out who was in favor and who was against the stadium bond issue. "Ray made it fun," Steadman said. "They wore caps, they'd ding a bell every time they found a voter for it, they cheered just like someone had hit a home run." The canvassers worked the phones 12 hours a day until they had called every home of a registered voter in Jackson County.

By election day they had a list of every voter who vowed to vote favorably. Over 100 Red Coaters spread out in high traffic locations around the county, handing out flyers that said, "Please Vote." And they went down the list of "yeas" and called with an offer for a ride. They dispatched cars to those who hadn't voted and didn't have a way to the polling place.

The issue passed with a 68.1 percent majority.

"You couldn't do that today any more than you could fly if you jumped out my window," Steadman said from his office, 15 floors above the city streets. "We had everything going right—outstanding team, Super Bowls, AFL-NFL merger, new baseball team, strong civic support, strong ticket sales—and we took advantage of the timing. But we wouldn't have made it even at that if it weren't for the efforts of the Chiefs Club leading up to the moment of the election. They made a big game out of it, and they won."

Arrowhead skeleton.

The Eventual Costs of Arrowhead

ALTHOUGH THE TRUMAN SPORTS COMPLEX project was built on a $43 million appropriation, the persons putting together the deal knew that it would take much more than that to have anything more than a bare-bones, no-frills finished product. That's why owners Lamar Hunt of the Chiefs and Ewing Kauffman of the Royals spent from their private coffers–$17.5 million between them–to include luxury suites, chairback seating, offices, stadium clubs, and other amenities that embellished an otherwise Spartan environment.

- In the final tally, the project cost totaled $69 million, plus the cost of land (bought by Jackson County), and roadways (paid for by Jackson County, the State of Missouri, and some federal funding), and the losses incurred from two labor strikes.

- The project drew $8.5 million from interest earned on the $43 million in bond money, some of which offset the strike losses.

- Hunt put $10 million into Arrowhead, covering the tab for the Gold Suite (Chiefs offices, the scoreboard and 80 luxury suites), among many extras, and Kauffman invested $7.5 million for enhancements of Royals Stadium, which now bears his name.

The appearance of over-indulgence into luxury created a stir with taxpayers until they learned that the club owners were footing the bill for such things as the chairback seats in the end zones, when the original plans called for bleachers. Don Fortune, a local radio-TV commentator who was among media representatives who toured the facilities during construction for updates and explanations of design, recalled, "A lot of hoopla was raised about all this opulence, including the suites, Lamar Hunt's private apartment, the press club (named later for the deceased, popular TV announcer Bruce Rice), and things in those days that were considered out of the ordinary and extravagant. Actually, it was ahead of its time. Today (25 years later) other cities want stadiums with suites. It was amazing foresight."

The only major error in overshooting the budget was the rolling roof that was part of the original concept. An engineer estimated it at $3.5 million, and by the time several plans were drawn (and rejected) the projected cost climbed to about $18.5. The novel idea was doomed by the cost …

Other costs were incurred after the fact at Arrowhead because of two mistakes:

- Water lines that encircled the stadium broke when the stadium in time shifted on its foundation.

- Waterproofing, which was scratched to save money during construction, was far more costly later when it became necessary.

Conversely, one item that was phased out to save money–escalators–proved to be a frugal decision in the long-term, too, because the Royals, who installed escalators, discovered them to be a terrible maintenance headache through the years.

Bill Love of the design firm Kivett-Myers said, "A comparable stadium today would cost between $150 million and $160 million. The $69 million cost of Arrowhead was an incredible bargain."

BACK-ROOM DEALS FOR A NEW FOOTBALL stadium took shape as the calendar flipped through 1966, and as summer heated up, Jack Steadman, who served as Lamar Hunt's dealer, received a call from Dutton Brookfield, a prominent figure from the Kansas City business world who was carrying the ball most for the public. The Chiefs wanted their own stadium, football configuration only, and preferably with a dome for protection against the dead of winter.

"None of the architectural suggestions were hitting home," Steadman recalled. "Dutton said some guy from Denver named Deaton was calling him and claiming to have the answer to our dome problem."

A domed stadium was fun to think about, talk about, given the attraction that the Astrodome in Houston had become, and given Kansas City's fickle winters that sometimes arrive in October. One of the most intriguing was the concept forwarded by Leon Brownfield, a Kansas City businessman. His wife's family owned the U-Smile Motel out on U.S. Highway 40 near where the Truman Complex eventually appeared, and across the street lay a maze of underground property that had been mined. Over lunch with Steadman, Brownfield excitedly suggested how a dome could be built over that area and eliminate the cost of air conditioning, because air circulated through the underground at a controlled, constant 55 degrees.

"It made sense," Steadman said. "We thought about a multipurpose stadium on that site." But, an architectural study revealed that the underground area wouldn't hold up under the weight of a domed stadium, so that wild idea dissolved.

Now, fast forward to Brookfield's call from Denver. Steadman said he would give a token 10-15 minutes to this man, Charles Deaton, who, it turned out, seemed like some kind of mad scientist in search of a lab where he could spring a brainchild on the world; rather, his ideas proved to be brilliant, and, to some degree, workable.

Reluctant, but relenting, Steadman invited Deaton to town and took him to the Kansas City Club for lunch. At first, he seemed normal. He presented a brochure and a portfolio of large projects he had created. "It was very attractive, actually," Steadman said. "He said he had been studying stadium projects, and he had a concept unlike anything anywhere. And he started drawing on a napkin...."

Spinning off of a footprint of Notre Dame's football stadium, which he considered to be the most ideal stadium in the world for watching football, Deaton sketched ways "to make it more beautiful" and how, without a dome, he could "weather-proof" it with a sliding roof. The moving cover, he said (heh, heh, heh), could protect both the baseball and the football stadia.

Steadman told him about Hunt's idea of having a space needle, fashioned after the one Seattle built for the World's Fair, and Deaton said no problem, he could build it, too. Deaton concluded, "I think we can do it within budget (two stadia, roof and needle)." Steadman recalled, "The more he talked, the more impressed I was," and he dispatched Deaton back to Denver to his drawing board with the charge to come up with a master plan. Deaton called back in a week. "I'm so excited!" he all but shrieked through the phone. Steadman was more than curious.

They met again, in Steadman's office. Seated at a conference table, Deaton broke out a large picture. "I called Dutton immediately, on the spot," Steadman said. "I said, 'This man has the damndest idea, and I've got to see you right now.' We met with Brookfield, and he said the same thing I did: 'Fantastic.' It was the sliding roof." Deaton had an engineer cost it out. The figures came back that the roof would cost $3.5 million.

The bond package was gaining steam. The Sports Authority convened to look at Deaton's wild idea, and their response to a man was, "We've got to do this." The sliding dome never happened, a major disappointment, but Deaton had won the heart of the dealmakers. However, the Sports Authority insisted that he partner with a local architectural firm. Deaton agreed, and he teamed with Kivett-Myers.

And Deaton's original design–the picture he

presented to Steadman–is what Arrowhead looks like. "He wouldn't budge one iota from it," Steadman said. "He was immovable when others wanted changes.

"I remember at first thinking he was kind of nuts, although very interesting, especially when he started talking about the moving roof and other benefits of a two-stadium project. Now, the stadium looks exactly like the conceptual drawing that he brought to us just a week after our original meeting. Charles Deaton, it turned out, was an amazing man with a great imagination."

The only major change from Deaton's schematic was no sliding roof. He had tried three different designs–one operating on rails with railroad car wheels, another using a water curtain to move it back and forth, and finally one using an air curtain. Final designs ran up to $18.5 million, however, scuttling the project.

Kansas City never did get its dome, or even its quasi-dome. It simply would have cost far too much, although as time marched on and domes appeared around the country, Kansas City often has looked back with regret at the bargain it would have been–even at five or six times the original bargain–basement estimate. Talks of some kind of roofing for Arrowhead still arise from time to time, and dollar signs always blur the vision.

The Gold Suite

ADISTINCTIVE SECTOR OF ARROWHEAD Stadium on the third and fourth floors is the Gold Suite, unique in its existence to house administrative offices and founder Lamar Hunt and his guests during Kansas City visits. Its interior design, resplendent in antiques and artwork, enhances its character even more.

Ward Haylett served as interior design consul-tant. "Because the suite was going to be 'our home' in Kansas City, we wanted some distinc-tive decor," Hunt said. "There are many interesting antiques." Among the most unusu-al is a wood carving hanging off a main wall at the top of a winding stairway. It depicts a lamb crozier and it came from a 16th Century cathedral in France. Lamar and his wife Norma bought it in a shop in Paris. "We were particularly taken by it, and it was hard to negotiate because we knew no French," he said. "Another customer who spoke English helped us out."

Every piece has a similar story behind it. The fireplace is one of Norma Hunt's favorites, also discovered in France. "It's ancient (17th Century), and it's so huge, it was perfect for the suite," she said, "It came in several pieces and was difficult to install. The construction crews were wonderful, so willing to help-it's a tribute to them. Remember, we opened Arrowhead incomplete (because of a labor strike), and the suite had bare concrete floors and temporary folding chairs. But the crew got the fireplace in, and showed their sense of humor. They tore off a small piece of a card-board box and cleverly placed it on top of the mantle with the words hand printed on it, 'See the 300-year-old Fireplace... Adults $5... Children $2!' It's one of a kind, extremely rare."

The fireplace is surrounded by eight 17th Century choir stalls obtained in Spain. Lamar Hunt found them indirectly as a result of a trip to find a coach for his Dallas Tornadoes of the old North American Soccer League. On a return trip, while searching the famous Rastro (flea market) in Madrid on a quest for a 14th Century choir book stand (that is now in their home), the Hunts purchased 24 of the elegant choir stalls that were in the same warehouse.

Several antique games, such as a skiddles table, occupy an upstairs anteroom. And an array of rare, collector's sports art prints hang on every wall. "Lamar inherited his mother's great love for antiquity and art," Norma Hunt said. The game room became a favorite hang-out of the Hunt's sons, Clark and Daniel–during Chiefs games! "I was upstairs

playing football more than I was down here watching it," Clark Hunt said, referring to one antique table football game. "Those games are really old, and I'm sure they're not meant to be played."

At every home game, the Hunts entertain dozens of special guests–politicians, sponsors, family friends, media, former players, even a couple who married in the parking lot in 1996. Norma Hunt is the quintessential hostess, greeting every guest by name. She has done her homework, learning something about the background of every guest. Assisting the Hunts in the chore of setting up pregame meals and halftime snacks are Wilma Wake, who was in her 20th year during the silver anniversary season, and Alice Clutter, in her 15th year. "It's like a big family up here, and we've seen all the little ones grow up," Wilma said. Alice added, "The Hunts are two of the

greatest people you'll ever know. They acknowledge everybody."

Diplomatically, Norma Hunt declined to single out guests any more distinguished than others, but she admitted to a special feeling for the various members of military service who have graced the premises–the Navy Seals parachute team, crews from the flyovers and Marines who collect Christmas Toys for Tots. And she said that the standing ovation for Sen. Thomas Eagleton of Missouri at the game that christened Arrowhead in 1972, soon after he was removed from Sen. George McGovern's presidential ticket, was memorable because " … he was so buoyed by that experience as he watched the game."

(Gold suite photos by Gary Carson)

33

Chapter 2 The Top 25: The Most Memorable Chiefs Games at Arrowhead

TO CREATE BOTH THE HEART AND BACKBONE of this 25th anniversary commemorative work, the author and publisher asked Chiefs owner Lamar Hunt to help us cull a list of the Top 25 memorable occasions at Arrowhead. Wow. Too many storied and historical moments remained after the first nominations, so we split into two parts— Chiefs games, and other events.

Even so, the choosing from all the 235 Chiefs games in the first 25 years—62 preseason, 170 regular season, and three playoffs—was a troublesome task, eliminating more than 90 percent of the action. Because even during some down seasons there were some isolated up plays, and games, and, most certainly, players. Some of those are covered elsewhere in recollections from

Some of the pre-game pageantry that christened the Chiefs '72 exhibition game against the Cardinals. (© Young Company).

former coaches and players and persons who have worked for the Chiefs, announcers and reporters, and fans.

The end result in this section is that Hunt and our staff couldn't hold it to 25, so you get a Top 26. Have fun second-guessing and debating us. You'll notice two striking trends: one is how hot the blood runs between the Chiefs and Raiders, with about one-third of the list comprising their classic matchups; two is that almost all of the list features victories. Certainly, for instance, nobody will ever forget the bummer that ended the 1995 season, the home loss to the Colts in the first round of playoffs that left a hollow feeling about the Chiefs' NFL-best 13-3 record. There were some prototypical Arrowhead Fever dates in 1996 that ended in a thud. But, hey, this project took life as a celebration, so it honors Hunt's contention that most of those games that turned out disfavoring Kansas City's team are, when you get right down to it, easy to blot from the mind. After all, you don't want to develop indigestion while you're reading.

The non-Chiefs events cover the unique appearances of the AFC-NFC Pro Bowl, Michael Jackson, Major League Soccer and other milestones of the entertainment world (and, in one case, the realm of religion, Promise Keepers), and remind us that Arrowhead also has played host to the unordinary, such as national championships of Drum and Bugle Corps, and tractor pull and monster truck competitions.

The events are listed chronologically. Enjoy.

Chiefs owner Lamar Hunt, who was inducted into the Pro Football Hall of Fame only 13 days before Arrowhead's grand opening, joined former Kansas City Mayor H. Roe Bartle for the fulfillment of the project that each of them only imagined five years earlier. During the pre-game ceremonies, Hunt declared Arrowhead Stadium open and a reality. (© Young Company).

The Governor's Cup was awarded annually to the winner of the Chiefs-Cardinals game from 1968-87. Since the Rams moved to St. Louis, the annual pre-season game again pits the two cities against each other for bragging rights resumed in 1996.
(© Young Company).

THE FIRST GAME: THE GOVERNOR'S CUP: AUG. 12, 1972
Attendance: 78,190
Chiefs 24, Cardinals 14 … Podolak christens the end zone … The 'Chief' made an appearance.

Arrowhead, although not 100 percent completed, welcomed the first crowd on Aug. 12, 1972. During the dedication ceremonies, the Governor's Cup was offered up to the winner of the preseason contest between the Chiefs and cross-state rival St. Louis, which became a tradition until the Cardinals moved to Phoenix in 1988. After a void of seven years, St. Louis obtained the Rams in a franchise move and the Governor's Cup game was renewed in 1996 for the opening of the 25th season in Arrowhead.

William Clarkson, the construction magnate who was one of the original members of the Jackson County Sports Authority, couldn't help but feel proud during a parade of dignitaries, including "Chief" H. Roe Bartle, in vintage automobiles prior to the kickoff. Bartle had been in ill health for several years.

"A great swan song for Roe Bartle and a wonderful standing ovation for Sen. Tom Eagleton in his first public appearance after being dropped as George McGovern's running mate in the presidential campaign," Clarkson said.

Ticket prices ranged from $10 for Club Level seats to $6 for end zone seats ($3 for children).

The Chiefs won their first game in their permanent home, 24-14, to the delight of 78,190 witnesses who had to be in awe of the surroundings. Larry Marshall returned a punt 75 yards on the most nerve-tingling play of the game. Ed Podolak, a college quarterback at Iowa who converted to halfback during his sterling Chiefs career, scored the first touchdown ever at Arrowhead.

Podolak remembered it vividly, 24 seasons later: "Oddly, what I remember most about it is that I got hurt on the play and had to sit out the next

few games," he said, laughing now at what wasn't a bit funny then.

Probably the most standout memory of the first game had nothing to do with what occurred on the field, but rather what occurred—and couldn't occur—in the stands. Delayed by two major labor strikes, the stadium construction wasn't complete. But team officials opened the gates anyway, utilizing makeshift barricades and extra security forces to keep curious persons out of dangerous areas. (Most agree that 25 years later the standards of OSHA and/or fire marshalls, etc., probably would have kept the doors shut until another day.) Temporary scaffolding and temporary stairwells helped make it possible to open on time.

Jim Schaaf, who was Public Relations Director at the time, said 25 years later, "I just remember the beauty of the stadium and the excitement of the fans. We didn't really realize until we got in it how beautiful it was. To this day, there's not a finer place in the NFL and it's been copied many times."

Ed Podolak (checkered sweater), walking off the field with Lamar Hunt, provided Chiefs fans with one of the most memorable individual performances in the history of the NFL in the last game at Municipal Stadium against the Miami Dolphins. He scored the last Chiefs touchdown ever at the old stadium, then scored the first touchdown ever at Arrowhead Stadium. (© Young Company).

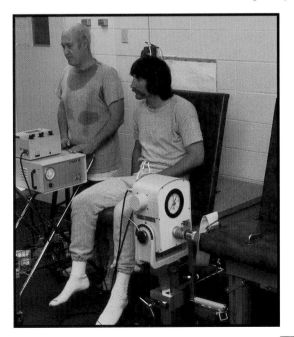

Recalling the first ever touchdown at Arrowhead, Ed Podolak said, "Oddly, what I remember most about it is that I got hurt on the play and had to sit out the next few games." (© Young Company)

Inside the Pipeline

Oops! Arrowhead's grand opening featured a grand closing of the drain pipes, and, consequently, of the restrooms. Amusing to look back on, but not the least bit funny at the time. Sometime during the third quarter of the Governor's Cup game against the St. Louis Cardinals, fans could no longer access the restrooms.

A combination of stuck valves and clogged drains wreaked havoc, creating a mini-flood from backed-up toilets. But the night was so sensational that the forgiving crowd scarcely let out a peep over the glitches that came with opening the stadium at about 85-90 percent complete. Ron Labinski, the lead architect representing Kivett and Myers at Arrowhead, remembered, "The ramp in one corner (northeast) wasn't finished, so we had firemen on duty to prevent problems."

Further, the temporary sound system was woefully weak, about 800 seats were still missing and suites weren't yet useable, and many concession areas and restrooms were incomplete. So the plumbing breakdown was merely a punctuation mark on this make-do night. Labinski explained how the sewers backed up because of uncleared debris from the construction work. "At the same time, on the water supply side, a lot of dirt caused the valves to stick open and let the water run constantly."

From that unfortunate situation Labinski, in his future years with another firm specializing in stadium construction, HOK Sports, devised a method to prevent its recurrence. Before the opening of any stadium he sends large crews throughout the facility to flush the toilets simultaneously, three times over, to make sure everything is clear and free from debris.

In keeping with a football theme, Labinski said, he refers to this practice as the "Super Flush."

Later in that first season, during a Nov. 19 game against the San Diego Chargers, Arrowhead experienced yet another shutdown of restroom facilities with a crowd of 79,011 on hand. Before the game, unbeknownst to them, a water main broke about 1/2 mile south of the stadium. Repair work cut off the stadium's water supply, and suddenly sinks, drinking fountains, toilets and showers ceased operation.

Harold Mack

This, on a near-freezing winter day when hot chocolate and coffee was gulped down in excess! Harold Mack, the longtime public address announcer, recalled thinking upon making the announcement just before halftime that restrooms were closed, "There are going to be a lot of boos, but there's going to be an awful lot of nervous giggles, too."

An early exodus followed, as the Chiefs became mired in a 29-19 loss to the Chargers. And the players' reward? Cold showers after the game.

RAIDER HATER I:
NOV. 5, 1972
Attendance: 82,094
Temp: 68
Chiefs 27, Raiders 14...
Lenny throws three, Jan gets his kicks...A changing of the guard, Lamonica to Snake...What's a sack?

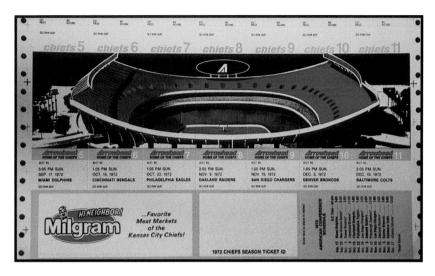

What could be more sweet than for the first regular-season victory at Arrowhead to come against the vile Oakland Raiders? Sweeter still because nine weeks had passed since a preseason win over the Dallas Cowboys, one of three preseason victories in the Chiefs new home. Oddly, Coach Hank Stram's defending AFC Western Division champions were 4-0 on the road, but 0-3 at Arrowhead as November dawned.

The office crowd was an all-time Arrowhead record because standing room only tickets could be sold in the early years. Raider hating already had become highly fashionable in Kansas City, fueled by an infamous spearing play involving the Raiders' Ben Davidson and the Chiefs' Len Dawson at Municipal Stadium and by the year-in, year-out heated battle for American Football League supremacy.

Furthermore, Raiders running back Marv Hubbard was quoted during the week that the Raiders were going to kick the Chiefs' rear.

So, this first Arrowhead visit by the Raiders stirred the blood and ranks as one of the all-time most memorable Chiefs dates at the new facility by virtue of a dominating 27-14 victory— "a proper beginning," as Lamar Hunt put it, "for our old AFL friends!"

In the face of a stiff wind (20-34 mph) the Chiefs jumped into 20-0 command on the arm of Dawson, the former Purdue star who threw touchdown passes to Wendell Hayes, Robert West and Ed Podolak. Hayes gathered Dawson's pass at the Raider 20 and dived over two defenders at the goal to complete the 29-yard play. The play to West covered 42 yards.

The ever-popular Podolak, one of the most memorable characters ever to don the Chiefs uniform, scored on a 27-yard play, part of a 157-yard day (115 rushing, 42 receiving). Dawson finished 10

Early days in the Arrowhead press-box. (© Young Company).

for 18, no interceptions, 181 yards, and three touchdown passes. After missing one field goal attempt wide right, Jan Stenerud was good from 31 and 40 yards, plus three PATs.

To the cry of "We want Hubbard! We want Hubbard", the Raiders running back couldn't gain enough yards to amount to a hill of beans.

Darryl Lamonica couldn't move the Raiders in the first half (9 for 15), so their rising future star, Kenny "Snake" Stabler took over and put some spark in Oakland's attack (14 for 23, 167 yards), repeatedly finding Fred Biletnikoff (10 catches, 114 yards). Phil Villapiano made 18 tackles for the Raiders, including 11 solo stops.

Three eventual Chiefs Hall of Famers head-lined the defense— linebacker Willie Lanier from Morgan State and linebacker Jim Lynch from Notre Dame with eight tack-les each, and tackle Buck Buchanan from Grambling with an important tackle for lost yardage on Stabler late in the game. Lynch also threw Stabler for minus 14 in the last series. Jim Marsalis led the Chiefs with nine tackles. Tackle Curley Culp, a collegiate heavyweight wrestling champion at Arizona State, and end Aaron Brown each caused Hubbard to fumble, one setting up a touchdown and the other a field goal.

Those lost-yardage plays by Buchanan and Lynch didn't count as sacks because the term and the statistic didn't exist until the following year, 1973.

Like the Chiefs, the

Raiders roster sparkled with names imbedded deep in the history of the rivalry, past and future: George Blanda was the placekicker; Art Shell, Gene Upshaw and Jim Otto anchored the interior line; Cliff Branch was about to blossom; Jack Tatum's notorious headhunting sustained the defense.

And, for perspective on the evolution of the game since Arrowhead opened, note that the Chiefs used just 12 substitutes, in addition to the two kickers. Six officials worked the game.

Against the Raiders, it wasn't difficult for the Chiefs Cheerleaders to pump up the fans. The Nov. 5, 1972 showdown against the Raiders stood as the most attended game in the first 25 years of Arrowhead when 82,094 fans gathered. (© Young Company).

Chapter 2

THE FIRST MATCHUP: THE 1972 CHIEFS STARTING LINEUPS

Offense

WR	Robert West, San Diego State
LT	Jim Tyrer, Ohio State
LG	Ed Budde, Michigan State
C	Jack Rudnay, Northwestern
RG	Mo Moorman, Texas A&M
RT	Dave Hill, Auburn
TE	Willie Frazier, Arkansas AM&N
WR	Otis Taylor, Prairie View
QB	Len Dawson, Purdue
RB	Ed Podolak, Iowa
RB	Wendell Hayes, Humboldt State

Defense

LE	Marvin Upshaw, Trinity
LT	Curley Culp, Arizona State
RT	Buck Buchanan, Grambling
RE	Aaron Brown, Minnesota
LLB	Bobby Bell, Minnesota
MLB	Willie Lanier, Morgan State
RLB	Jim Lynch, Notre Dame
LCB	Jim Marsalis, Tennessee State
RCB	Emmitt Thomas, Bishop College
LS	Jim Kearney, Prairie View
RS	Mike Sensibaugh, Ohio State
PK	Jan Stenerud, Montana State
P	Jerrel Wilson, Southern Mississippi

Substitutes

Mike Adamle, RB, Northwestern... Larry Marshall, DB/KR, Maryland... Nate Allen, CB, Texas Southern... Mike Oriard, C, Notre Dame...Clyde Werner, LB, Washington...George Daney, G, Texas El Paso...Bob Stein, LB, Minnesota... George Seals, DT, Missouri...Sid Smith, T, Southern Cal...Jim Otis, RB, Ohio State...Morris Stroud, TE, Clark... Wilbur Young, DE, William Penn. (Did Not Play: Dean Carlson, QB, Iowa State... Mike Livingston, QB, Missouri... Elmo Wright, WR, Houston...Jeff Kinney, RB, Nebraska)

The Officials

Referee	Pat Haggerty
Umpire	Al Conway
Line Judge	Dean Look
Linesman	Walt Peters
Back Judge	Ralph Vandenberg
Field Judge	Pat Mallette

The days leading up to a Chiefs game against the Raiders became ceremonial across Kansas City–"Raider Hater" week. Workers everywhere don red clothing, often replete with a Chiefs logo. The emotions stirred by the rivalry go all the way back to AFL days, before Arrowhead Stadium, heightened by the infamous Davidson spearing of beloved quarterback Len Dawson.

Arrowhead most likely never will hold a crowd any larger than the 1972 Raiders game that attracted 82,094 whose reward was the Chiefs' first-ever regular season victory, 27-14, on Nov. 5. (That was before standing-room-only tickets were suspended.)

Chiefs head coach Marty Schottenheimer got caught up in the intense rivalry very quickly after arriving in Kansas City in 1989. His first home game: the Raiders. He was well aware of their game at Arrowhead the year before that erupted into a helmet-swinging melee during a 27-17 Raiders victory. Thoughts of that game got Schottenheimer's blood boiling.

"I mean, that was ugly," he said during his weekly meeting with reporters before the 1996 Raiders game. "It was very obvious to me even before we got here that these two teams were going to go tooth-and-nail, toe-to-toe, and play the entire game to its verdict."

The Chiefs won, and for eight straight seasons they won at Arrowhead over the arch enemy Raiders, and lost but twice to them on the road. "The rivalry is what makes the National Football League great," Chiefs president Carl Peterson told the 1996 "Red Friday" luncheon crowd before the home opener against the Raiders. "A tradition that our young players are thrilled about and excited about. Our coaches, everyone in this organization, every-one in this community. This is a fun, great week for all of us."

That 1996, 25th anniversary Raiders home game ended in a 19-3 victory that helped cata-pult the Chiefs to their first 4-0 start in team history.

During a summer practice before the '81 season, Chiefs General Manager Jim Schaaf and Coach Marv Levy observed a pair of rookies who made an impact in Chiefs history, Lloyd Burruss and Joe Delaney, two of the Chiefs' top five picks in the draft that year. Delaney was chosen in the second round out of Northwest Louisiana and Burruss was the third of three picks the Chiefs had in the third round. (© Young Company)

RAIDER HATER II: OCT. 11, 1981
Attendance: 76,543
Temp: 69

Chiefs 27, Raiders 0... Tremendous trenches...Rookie runs rampant... Raiders blankety—blank-blank.

This victory was "Marv"elous—one of erstwhile Coach Marv Levy's finest hours in his short reign with the Chiefs. The offensive line received game balls, sensational first-year running back Joe Delaney out of Northwest Louisiana gained the equivalent of more than two lengths of the field, and the Raiders, coming off of a Super Bowl year, incurred their third shutout in a row.

The largest home crowd in nine years, since the very first year in Arrowhead, turned out for the annual Raider Hater gala. The Chiefs entered the season with their offense bolstered by the rookie Delaney (who died two years later in an off-season drowning accident) and an unproven quarterback, Bill Kenney, who at one time had been a tight end at Northern Colorado. He had guided the team to two victories in the last three games of 1980 after Steve Fuller, the supposed QB of the future as a No. 1 draft pick out of Clemson, sustained an injury.

Delaney and Kenney sparked this thorough whipping of the notorious Raiders, part of the push to the Chiefs' first winning season in eight years (9-7), and a third-place finish in the Western Division. This day represented an apogee of optimism, a shining beacon in the Levy era of encouragement and gradual improvement—all of which came crashing down the next year under the strain of a player strike and crumbling record (2-6).

Levy went on much later to take the Buffalo Bills to four Super Bowls, and the Chiefs had to wade through four years, a new city (Los Angeles), and five losses before they beat the Raiders again (see Raider Hater III).

Kenney, who earned his way up from third-team quarterback under Levy, passed for 287 yards (15 for 23), and 104 went to Delaney on three catches, including a 61-yard catch and run. Henry Marshall, a favorite with University of Missouri fans, made six catches for 110 yards, and he and J.T. Smith caught short touchdown passes, prompting Levy to remark, "They are two classy receivers."

With the kickoff temperature at 69 degrees for the Oct. 11 game against the Raiders, Chiefs fans experienced a perfect Indian summer day on an autumn afternoon. (© Young Company)

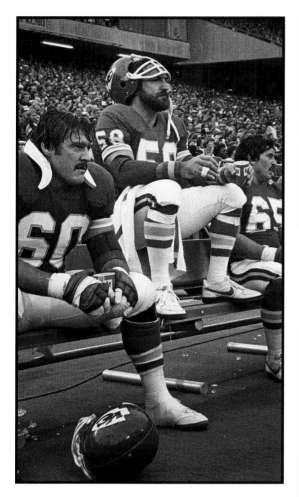

Center Jack Rudnay (#58) anchored an offensive line that linemate Tom Condon said was much-maligned only one season earlier. Against the Raiders, each member of the offensive line received a game ball after helping the Chiefs offense successfully move the ball in their 27-0 win over the Raiders.
(© Young Company)

In the war room room for the 1978 draft, the Chiefs prepared to take two defensive players who proved to be key factors in some of the biggest games at Arrowhead in the ensuing years. Defensive end Art Still was the top choice and linebacker Gary Spani, the Kansas State All-American, was a third round choice.
(© Young Company)

With Mike Bell and Art Still (#67) anchoring the Chiefs defensive line, the Raiders were held to a scoreless effort and to 79 yards rushing, a season in which the Chiefs ranked first in the AFC against the run. Bell finished the season as the team's third leading tackler and second in sacks. (© Young Company)

He also praised Delaney: "The little guy is a great competitor. He has a lot of ability and he works damn hard. He's willing to work, and he's worked hard since the day he came here."

As a second-round draft choice, Delaney carried speed as his main asset because at 5-10 and 184 pounds, one had to wonder how much pounding he could absorb in the NFL. The fans at Arrowhead didn't know what they were in for.

Tom Condon, the 11-year veteran guard, reflected on Delaney in an interview ten years after Delaney's last NFL season ('82).

"Joe was such a great guy. He was always the first player in the locker room everyday and he wasn't very big. But he had such a sinewy body and he was just rippling muscles."

Delaney carried 28 times for 106 yards, his second straight game over 100. "If the line plays the way they did today," he said, "I'll get 100 every time." Levy concurred. Levy liked giving out game balls, and for this game he gave one to each of the offensive linemen:

• Left tackle Matt Herkenhoff (Minnesota);

• Left guard Brad Budde (Southern Cal), the 1980 No. 1 draft pick whose father, Ed, is in the Chiefs Hall of Fame after playing the same position 14 years, 11 as a starter;

Steve Fuller was the second choice in the first round of the 1979 draft, but by 1981, lost his starting job to Bill Kenney, who responded with a big game against the Raiders. Fuller didn't regain the starting job until the final three games of the '81 season. (© Young Company)

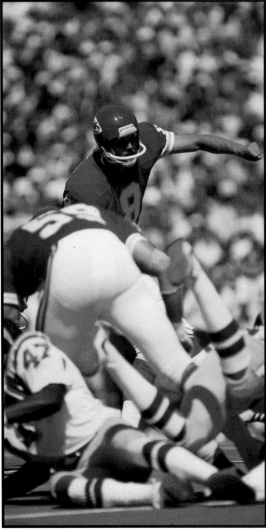

Against San Diego in the preceding home game before the Chiefs-Raiders showdown, Nick Lowery was prepping for a big boot. The '81 Raider game featured Lowery's longest field goal of the season when he split the uprights from 52 yards out. Throughout his career with the Chiefs (1980-93), Lowery kicked eight 52-yard field goals. Five others were longer, including his career best from 58 yards on two occasions. In 1981, Lowery was selected to his first Pro Bowl. (© Young Company)

- Center Jack Rudnay (Northwestern), a Chiefs Hall of Famer who anchored the middle of the line for 13 seasons;

- Right guard Tom Condon (Boston College), who later became an attorney representing the NFL Players Association, and then joined renowned IMG as an agent;

- Right tackle Charlie Getty (Penn State);

- Tight end Al Dixon (Iowa State).

The same core, according to Condon, absorbed even more abuse than just in the game. "They talked about us in the newspaper as an average offensive line, that they had to start replacing people, and 'we couldn't get the job done' and all that kind of thing. The next year, we have Joe Delaney and he starts after the first quarter of the season, gains over 1,000 yards, goes to the Pro Bowl, and that year they talked about us as a dominating offensive line," Condon said.

The line laid the foundation for an expertly balanced attack against such notorious defenders as Ted "The Stork" Hendricks, Matt Millen and Rod Martin.

Oakland's offense that the Chiefs shut down featured quarterback Jim Plunkett, a former Heisman Trophy winner at Stanford; his favorite target Cliff Branch, an Olympic sprinter from Colorado who was one of the fastest receivers ever to grace the NFL, and Art Shell blocking up front, not realizing that one day he would be coaching first the Raiders and, 14 years after this game, the Chiefs' offensive line.

Leading the swarming Chiefs defense, linebacker Whitney Paul, cornerback Eric Harris and safety Gary Barbaro intercepted Plunkett. Cal Peterson made eight tackles and Gary Spani, a local favorite because of his Kansas State background, made six from linebacking spots, as Oakland managed just 79 rushing yards and 129 in the air. "It's the best we've played all year," Levy said, as Kansas City's record moved to 4-2. "We're a serious contender."

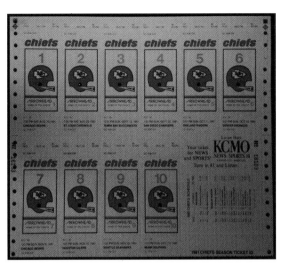

DELANEY DUNS THE OILERS: NOV. 15, 1981
Attendance: 73,984
Temp: 61

Chiefs 23, Oilers 10 ... Record-book running (193) ... Snake again ... Heisman Who?

Ken "Fuzzy" Kremer (left) and Tom Condon, two ex-teammates who battled in the trenches on opposite sides of the line of scrimmage, are now working as partners in the player representation field. Kremer was one of three players who received game balls in the Chiefs' '81 win over the Houston Oilers. Condon was responsible for opening daylight that allowed Joe Delaney to pick his seams in a record-setting performance.
(© Young Company)

The 1981 season held so much promise. Joe Delaney created more excitement than any ball carrier since the glorious pre-Arrowhead days of Abner Haynes and Mike Garrett. The team got off to a rousing 6-2 start, but by the time the Oilers rolled into town Chiefs fans were finicky over two straight losses—by two points at San Diego, and by three at home against the Bears.

Delaney electro-charged the fans with a dazzling array of runs that carried the Chiefs to a convincing victory, and carried him into the Chiefs' record book for yards rushing in a single game, 193, on just 23 carries. The faithful thought this would be a springboard back into the playoffs for the first time in eons, especially after the Chiefs pummeled the Seahawks the following week 40-13 (and a mere 49,002 turned out!).

Cornerback Eric Harris (#44) and Wide Receiver J.T. Smith were two key performers for the Chiefs in 1981. Harris tied for second in the AFC in interceptions with seven, including one in the Chiefs' 23-10 win over the Houston Oilers. Smith was selected to the Pro Bowl the previous season as a punt returner, but led the team in receptions in '81. Harris received a game ball in the Chiefs win over the Oilers.
(© Young Company)

The game *was* a springboard—for Delaney to finish as the franchise's one-season rushing leader at the time with 1,121 yards on 234 carries ... but the Chiefs lost three in a row, and only a victory over the Vikings in Minnesota on the last day of the season preserved a winning season (9-7). As it turned out, Delaney enjoyed but two seasons in a Chiefs uniform; trying to save three children in a lake near his hometown Monroe, La., he tragically drowned during the summer of 1983.

"The Oiler game was sensational," said former offensive lineman Tom Condon. "I'd never been in

After arriving in Kansas City as a seventh round draft choice, Ken Kremer went to become the Chiefs leader in sacks in 1981. Against the Oilers, Kremer sacked Kenny Stabler twice for 17 yards in losses. He finished the year with eight sacks for 57 yards in losses.
(© Young Company)

Until Jack Rudnay missed the first four games of the 1980 season with a torn hamstring, he played in 144 consecutive games. By the '81 season, Rudnay was in his 12th season and in his fifth as team captain. (© Young Company)

a game like that before. Joe was a special guy. He had unbelievable talents and it's just hard to believe that he was taken so quickly."

"Joe's performance was magnificent," Marv Levy said after the record-setting Oilers game, but his words carried over, applying to the athlete and the person for all time. "People expect too much from rookies, and rookies don't expect enough from themselves"—a favorite Levy homily—"but that does not apply to Joe Delaney. He is a fantastic worker, and fantastic person."

Besides carrying the team on his back at 6.7 yards a carry (longest gain, 26), Delaney carried in one touchdown from 6 yards out. The other running back in Levy's unordinary Wing-T, ground-based offense, Billy Jackson, carried the second touchdown in from the 1. Nick Lowery kicked field goals of 37, 42 and 38 yards. Fullback James Hadnot carved out 47 yards as the team compiled 258 on the ground, while quarterback Bill Kenney attempted just 11 passes and gained 39 yards on six completions.

Facing an old nemesis in his twilight years, the Chiefs limited Snake Stabler to 10 for 17 passing in relief of John Reaves, but one connected with Ken Burrough for a 50-yard touchdown. Levy awarded game balls to three defenders—cornerback Eric Harris, who made two interceptions and recovered a fumble, safety Lloyd Burruss and nose tackle Ken "Fuzzy" Kremer. Also contributing big plays on defense were cornerback Gary Green, who intercepted a pass, and free safety Gary Barbaro, who smothered a fumble.

"Our game plan revolved around stopping Earl Campbell and our kickoff coverage, which was superb," Levy said. He said the special teams "swarmed…(and) played with inspiration," naming Phil Cancik, Curtis Bledsoe, and Ed Beckman. Campbell, the former Heisman winner at Texas, gained 99 yards on 21 carries, but didn't score and was lost in the shadows of Delaney's feat.

After the game, Delaney's comments, as he held a game ball in his hands, reflected the personality that stamped him forever with Chiefs comrades—self-assured but humble: "I don't mind being the guy the team counts on. I don't think about it. I just work hard, do the best I can, and try to do things right. I want to go out and be a good team man and win the game. Yards don't mean that much to me, just winning. I'll carry the ball as many times as I have to for us to get the job done… it doesn't matter how many carries it takes."

"You could see that he was always enthusiastic about just being there, and excited about being a rookie and being on the team," Condon said "But he didn't act like a rookie usually where they're typically reticent and want to hang back a little bit. No, he was a real effervescent guy."

For the first time in NFL history, the same team chose a father and a son in the first round when the Chiefs chose Ed Budde ('63) and Brad Budde ('80). By Brad Budde's second season, he improved enough to stabilize an offensive line that helped the Chiefs finish first in the AFC in rushing. Not only did the 1981 offensive line help Joe Delaney find the holes, but reduced by 20 the number of quarterback sacks from the previous season. (© Young Company)

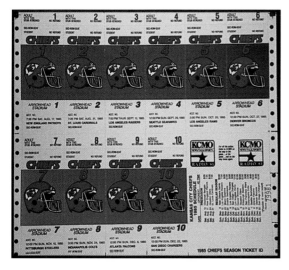

RAIDER HATER III THROUGH THE EYES OF ABC: SEPT. 12, 1985
Attendance: 72,686
Temp: 72

Chiefs 36, Raiders 20...(Lowery's) Foot, Lewis and fancy free...Carson on the corners...A slug-out, no bull.

This one turned out to be an "only"—the only time the Chiefs beat the Raiders at Arrowhead in Coach John Mackovic's four opportunities. Once more, Chiefs fans were caught in a tease at the time. Just four days earlier in the season opener, QB Bill Kenney's three TD passes and 397 yards and Nick Lowery's 4-for-4 field goal effort buried the Saints 47-27 in New Orleans.

Bring on the Darth Vaders! They were in their fourth year in Los Angeles—it still sounds unnatural...Los Angeles Raiders—and they had beaten the Chiefs five consecutive times since the Chiefs' 1981 sweep before the Raiders left Oakland. At the core of the Raiders team was the makeup of a team that won the Super Bowl only two seasons earlier, while the Chiefs appeared to be stepping forward under third-year coach John Mackovic. In Mackovic's rookie season, the Chiefs finished at 6-10 before improving to 8-8 in '84.

Bill Maas, a number one draft choice out of Pittsburgh, was a rookie noseguard in '84, a season without any primetime exposure, so he relished with delight the chance to play a high caliber Raider team. "It was a Who's Who of everybody in football that you were playing against and it was a big step for us as a Chiefs franchise," Mass said.

Former Chiefs running back Theotis Brown, whose NFL career was cut short a year earlier by heart trouble, returned to the field for the singing of the national anthem prior to the 1985 Chiefs home opener against the Raiders.
(© Young Company)

Chiefs tight end Walt Arnold helped Coach John Mackovic capture his first win against the Raiders at Arrowhead by turning in a career night. Arnold, who started in '85 and '86, caught four passes for 69 yards, which was a career high.
(© Young Company)

Henry Marshall's '85 season was cut short by a shoulder separation, but the Chiefs all-time leader in career pass receptions snared four catches for a season-high 90 yards against the Raiders. In the first half of the season, Marshall was the Chiefs leading receiver until the injury sidelined him in the NFL's Week 9. (© Young Company)

Super-revved, the superlative crowd thrilled to a double comeback. The Chiefs trailed 7-0 and 14-9 before reeling off 27 straight points—including an Arrowhead record by Lowery—that pushed them to a 2-0 start. Subsequently the season fizzled, but for this one night the whole country dropped into Arrowhead and witnessed NFL football at its most feverish. The only shroud lingering through one grandiose night of Raider-Hater mania was the haze of smoke from grills in the parking lots—one of football's most renowned tailgate settings.

"We got our (behinds) kicked tonight," Raiders defensive whiz Howie Long said to a throng of reporters after the game.

Kenney took up where he left off in New Orleans, gaining 259 air yards on 18 for 38 accuracy—giving him 656 yards on 40 completions just five days into the season. "He played like a Pro Bowler," Raiders defensive end Lyle Alzado said. (Kenney had been in the all-star game the year before, but he never returned.)

Carlos Carson caught five for 118 yards, including a 25-yard TD. Long said of Kenney, "When the

money was on the line he put the ball on the mark." Raiders cornerback Lester Hayes tried to leave his mark on Carson. They scuffled. "He grabbed my face mask," Carson said. "I told him I didn't appreciate it. He apologized later. That's part of the game. We worked on the corners. Instead of speeding off the ball, the receivers got together as a group and decided to make them commit. It worked."

Nick Lowery's foot provided the catalyst for victory. He kicked true from 39, 22, and 42 yards and gave the Chiefs their first lead, 9-7. He then hit from 58—the longest field goal ever at Arrowhead—and 21 that regained the lead for good at 15-14. "It's amazing how those three-pointers add up," said Lowery, who eventually added them up higher than any kicker in history with the Chiefs and Jets. Scoring passes to wide receivers Carson (25 yards) and Stephone Paige (5 yards) secured third-quarter control.

Cornerback Albert Lewis was a highly popular Chief with his 38 career interceptions (twice he picked three in one game, both times against the Falcons), but years later he became a "turncoat" as a free agent and returned to Arrowhead wearing a Raiders uniform! In this game, though, he inflicted much damage on the Raiders. He and Sherman Cocroft made interceptions. And Lewis hammered the coffin shut by falling on a fumble in the end zone for a touchdown.

Maas (teammates referred to him as "Billy Bob") made two sacks on Jim Plunkett and forced a fumble.

"That made it memorable for me," Maas said.

Plunkett's fumble was recovered by Art Still, who also had a sack that added to his all-time team record, 72.5, that held up until the Derrick Thomas-Neil Smith era. The Plunkett-Marcus Allen offense never got on track, running into 18 tackles by the safeties—10 by Lloyd Burruss, eight by Deron Cherry, an eventual Chiefs Hall of Famer after begging Marv Levy for the chance to play. Cornerback Kevin Ross also recovered a fumble.

Lewis saw a breakthrough. Since joining the Chiefs as a third-round draftee, he had suffered four straight Raider defeats by margins of 1, 9, 2 and 10. He said, "In the past we slugged it out with the Raiders for eight rounds. Tonight we slugged it out for 10."

Long summed it up: "Sometimes you get the bull, sometimes the bull gets you."

CHERRY PICKING:
SEPT. 29, 1985
Attendance: 50,485
Temp: 47
Chiefs 28, Seahawks 7...Done in by Deron...Crowd swells... Hope crashes and burns.

E.J. Jones, who made the Chiefs as a free agent running back from the University of Kansas, picked up 12 of his 19 total rushing yards on the season against the Seahawks. (© Young Company)

After a shutout setback at Miami, this 28-7 victory over Seattle at Arrowhead bore significance for several reasons. For one, it showed resiliency after a stunning 31-0 loss against the Dolphins. It made the record 3-1. For another, attendance rose. Counting preseason, the club was 6-2, and anticipation rose to heights they hadn't reached for ages. Crowds swelled from the dismal lows of so many years.

Most memorable, though, were the eye-popping exploits of safety Deron Cherry. A fifth-year veteran from Rutgers, he made four interceptions—tying the NFL record and clipping the Seahawks' wings severely.

"The one thing I remember was, of course, catching the four balls, but I also remember not catching the five other times I had my hands on the ball," Cherry said, he picked off three passes thrown by Dave Krieg, who, unbeknownst to both, would one day become a Chief one day.

"It was a wet and rainy day, real sloppy. We were able to get out front of Seattle early in the game which forced them to change their game plan," said Cherry, the third-ranked interception leader in Chiefs history (Emmitt Thomas and Johnny Robinson rank 1-2 respectively). "Seattle loved to run the football and we forced them out of that type of game plan where they had to pass to catch up. Because of the weather conditions, it's a lot easier playing the secondary when you could just sit back there and roam knowing that the quarterback has got to throw the ball."

Cherry kept all four footballs as a remembrance, but had room for a fifth that would have allowed him to stand alone in the NFL record book. "I had two or three legitimate chances at catching a couple more, but the conditions were bad and they just slipped through my hands," Cherry said.

Undrafted in 1981 and signed for a tryout as a punter, Cherry talked Levy into an opportunity to play in the secondary. Two years later he became a fixture in the lineup. He added six more seasons to his extraordinary career, and during the 25th

anniversary season of Arrowhead he entered the Chiefs Hall of Fame.

"I boosted his career totals for interceptions, I think between me and Elway, he's got about 80 percent of his interceptions," said Krieg, who had several nightmares at Arrowhead Stadium before joining the Chiefs in 1992.

So the Chiefs were riding high at this point of '85. And then, ka-BOOM! That crash you heard was the Chiefs tumbling back into the abyss with a seven-game losing streak.

Stephone Paige, though pressed into duty as a starter because of the shoulder injury to Henry Marshall, was regarded as one of the best third-down receivers in the NFL. Of his 59 catches on third down in '85, 50 went either for a first down or a touchdown. (© Young Company)

NEW PAIGE IN THE RECORD BOOK: DEC. 22, 1985

Attendance: 18,178
Temp: Sub-freezing

Chiefs 38, Chargers 34...40-year NFL reception record rent asunder...a $1,000 signee...The crowd was barren and brrrr-in'.

The season had fallen dark. Five-and-10, buried under the rest of the West. One thing was for certain. An NFL record was going to fall.

Lionel "Train" James of the San Diego Chargers was on the verge of breaking a record that was set ten years earlier by Terry Metcalf of the St. Louis Cardinals for all-purpose yardage in one season. He did, but another NFL record fell that overshadowed James' performance.

A beacon was sorely needed for the Chiefs. Stephone Paige, a third-year player out of Fresno State, provided light, brilliant light, and then some. Starting because of a shoulder separation injury to incumbent Henry Marshall, Paige hauled in passes from Todd Blackledge and Bill Kenney all over the field, Paige mustered 309 yards, an NFL record for one game, on just eight catches.

"It was one of those days when everything went right. I mean everything," Paige said. "That was a day I'll never forget. It seemed like that was my

Otis Taylor, (#89) played from 1965 to 1975 and remains the Chiefs all-time leader in touchdown receptions with 57. Chris Burford is second with 55 and Stephone Paige is third with 49. (© Young Company)

time, that it was my day and it happened to me."

No matter which quarterback took the snap, Paige was glue when the ball was stuck in his numbers. The performance propelled the Chiefs to a 38-34 victory over the Chargers, who weren't terrific, but nonetheless stood three games ahead of the Chiefs going into the game. Conditions couldn't have been more bleak: the Chiefs were steadfast in dead last, the attendance was a paltry 18,178, attributable not only to another season frittered away, but also to temperatures only an Eskimo could love.

"I remember it was cold," Paige said.

"I remember it so well because of how good I felt for Stephone," John Mackovic said from his office in Austin, Tex., where he coaches the Texas Longhorns after an interim stop at Illinois. "But also because of the time of year. We were out of contention, and it was bitter cold."

Paige's record production broke a standard that withstood 40 years of NFL pass-catching, established in 1945 by Jim Benton. "That was more fun watching him," Mackovic said. "Here was a kid who we signed for a $1,000 bonus, and he probably would have signed for less because he always wanted to play for the Chiefs."

Curtis McClintan held the old Chiefs record for receiving yardage in one game – five catches for 213 yards against Denver in 1965.

"I really didn't know about any records. I just said, 'Hey, this is the most fun I ever had in the NFL,' " Paige said, who had already broken the team record by halftime when compiling 258 receiving yards. Marshall, who still holds the Chiefs all-time record for career pass receptions, informed Paige that he shattered the team record.

In the first quarter, Paige caught a 56-yard pass and a 51-yarder, both for touchdowns, from starting quarterback Todd Blackledge. The second quarter wasn't as Chiefs friendly as Blackledge suffered a dislocated thumb that sidelined him for the rest of the game and Paige missed most of the quarter with bruised ribs.

After the kind of numbers Paige posted in the opening half, he thought he would see something other than the single coverage the Chargers played against him in the first 30 minutes. He was shocked to find that there was no change.

"Every time I lined up, they played the same way. There would be one guy there and nobody would

help that guy out, so I just remember getting open and running," Paige said. Before that game, Paige never had a 100-yard receiving day in the NFL.

Paige remained a starter for six years, and his record lasted four years. Willie "Flipper" Anderson of the Rams broke Paige's record with 336 yards against the Saints in 1989. Although Anderson's achievements erased Paige's day of glory from the NFL record books, Stephone has another Paige in the Chiefs record book: starting in November, 1985, Paige made a catch in a club record 83 consecutive games over the next six years.

PICKING ELWAY APART: DEC. 7, 1986
Attendance: 47,019
Temp: 45, light rain
Chiefs 37, Broncos 10...On blitzin'!...The I's have it..."He's only human."

Pete Koch started all 16 games for the Chiefs on the defensive line in '86. Against Denver, he played two of his best games. After a team-leading ten tackle effort at Denver, Koch deflected two pass attempts to go along with 1 sack and five tackles. (© Young Company)

"Just three weeks to go," John Mackovic said to his huddled team at a meeting before the game, "and we have to win all three. A lot of people have given up on you. I haven't. We can do it."

Atop the AFC West at the time were the Broncos at 10-3, three games ahead of the Chiefs, 7-6, who were mired in a three-game losing streak. If there was a silver lining, the Chiefs were 5-2 at Arrowhead, their best record there since 1973 when the team went 5-1-1.

And, lo, the Chiefs finally turned a long-awaited, much-abated corner, and this game was the pivot step for the new, upwardly-mobile direction—a 37-10 thrashing of hearty old rival Denver. Such a rarity: Elway, typically ramming a defeat down Chiefs throats in the waning minutes of games through the years, with no zip on his passes resulting in zip on the scoreboard.

The Chiefs weren't about to let this Pearl Harbor anniversary pass bleakly, despite a light rain that added chill to a dreary day. They operated out of a set of new blitzes, interspersed with fake blitzes. "Between the two of those strategies," Mackovic recalled, "we were on him from the very beginning." The results: three interceptions and five sacks of Elway, and one interception of his sub, Gary Kubiak.

The offense also switched some formations and, buffered by great field position from defensive gems, racked up touchdown passes from Todd Blackledge to Stephone Paige and Jeff Smith, and a 1-yard dive by Green. Nick Lowery added three field goals on six attempts.

Lloyd Burruss capped the day appropriately enough with a 72-yard TD return of an interception. Gary Spani, Sherman Cocroft, Scott Radecic and Deron Cherry also made interceptions. Pete Koch, an erstwhile actor who grabbed attention off the field with a role in "Heartbreak Ridge," a Clint Eastwood movie about the Marines, and Lewis Cooper had 1 sack each, and Art Still and Cherry each had one. Kevin Ross made nine tackles. Koch said afterward, "Elway (who scored a TD) is dangerous, but he's only a human being."

"They (the Broncos) were good," said Frank Gansz, who was the assistant head coach and special teams coach at the time. "But Deron Cherry always played real well against them and our defense played great. We made some plays and we just outplayed them."

Gansz sensed something special from that final home game. "Any time you have a divisional opponent, it was huge there. I think because there was so much on the line in the season, it was big for everybody." he said.

The victory, shocking in its lopsidedness, provided an invigorating wake-up call. Despite the tie with Seattle for third place in the AFC West, the Chiefs went into the game as one of eight AFC teams left with hopes of making the playoffs.

"We treated it like a playoff game," Mackovic said, "and pulled out all the stops with new formations

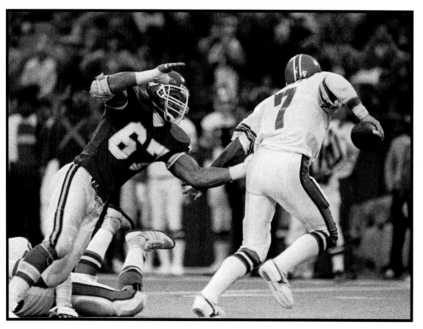

Art Still, seen pursuing Denver quarterback John Elway, played every defensive down in '86. When he was selected by the Chiefs as the second overall pick in the '78 NFL Draft, only Earl Campbell was chosen ahead of him. (© Young Company)

both ways." The head coach praised his staff of assistants before the media after the game—"they do not get enough credit"—and referred to the defense as "magnificent" and Blackledge's effort as "a superior game—the best he's played for us." The quarterback from Penn State was in his fourth season after becoming a No. 1 draft pick in 1983.

Oddly, in a 37-point output, there were no big individual numbers in the Chiefs' meager 169-yard output (compared to Denver's 323). Henry Marshall made his 400th career reception, closing in on Otis Taylor's team record 410. "Looking at the game stats may not be exciting to fans," Mackovic said, "but to us it's totally exciting."

The main result was the team's renewed outlook. "If we're clicking," said Paige, who made his 10th TD catch of the season, "when we're on, nobody can beat us." And nobody else did. Confidence restored, the team did a 180-degree turnaround, swinging from three consecutive losses to three consecutive wins.

The Denver debacle at Arrowhead set the table: a first-ever victory at Los Angeles Coliseum followed, 20-17 over the Raiders, and yet another road victory, 24-19 at Pittsburgh, catapulted the Chiefs into a wild card spot. Christmas came four days early for Chiefs fans who found their heroes in the playoffs, ending a 15-year absence from the championship chase. Just 47,019 were on hand to witness, some of whom are suspected of sustaining lingering soreness from pinching themselves.

Like a year earlier, Stephone Paige turned it up a notch in December. He scored the Chiefs first touchdown against the Broncos in their must-win game. In the final 11 games, Paige caught eight of his 11 TD passes on the year. (© Young Company)

Carlos Carson, who still led the Chiefs in average yards per catch in '86 despite missing nearly half the season with injuries, returned to form the next season. The year with the theme "Sic'em Chiefs." (© Young Company)

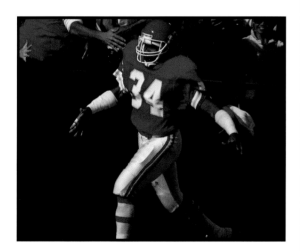

Strong safety Lloyd Burruss earned his first Pro Bowl berth from his performance in '86. Of five interceptions on the season, three were returned for touchdowns, including the 72-yard TD return against the Broncos at Arrowhead. A year earlier, Burruss earned team MVP honors. (© Young Company)

Under fire for selecting Todd Blackledge in the 1983 draft, John Mackovic turned to him when the Chiefs' playoffs hopes were on the line against Denver in '86. When replacing the injured Bill Kenney, Blackledge responded by completing 14 of 29 passes with no interceptions and two touchdowns. (© Young Company)

Chiefs defensive coordinator Walt Corey provided some inspiration for the Chiefs defensive line to keep the pressure turned up on Bengals quarterback Boomer Esiason.
(© Young Company)

THE "HIDDEN GUEST": NOV. 13, 1988
Attendance: 34,614
Temp: 59
Chiefs 31, Bengals 28...Loweryng the boom...Spying eyes.

In a game loaded with memories, the Chiefs came from nine behind and won with 12 points in the last six minutes.

"We had some real big plays and they were a great team, one of the best teams in the league," said Frank Gansz, who enjoyed his finest hour as a Chiefs head coach. The Bengals entered the game with a 8-2 record in what turned out to be a Super Bowl season.

Nick Lowery capped a 5-for-5 day when he won it with a clock beating field goal against a team with such stars as left tackle dancing Anthony Munoz and kick returner Ickey Woods (his entertaining "Ickey Shuffle" amused fans after touchdowns), and quarterback Boomer Esiason.

But the most significant part of the day, ultimately, didn't become publicly known until now: A guest for the game, invited by Lamar Hunt, was Carl Peterson. He roamed about, hidden in the crowd of 34,614 as he "scouted" the Chiefs and the organization to see, as Hunt put it, "if he really wanted to get involved."

Peterson could bask in an unseasonably warm, sunshiny day, and in some semblance of Chiefs glory as they put up 418 yards of balanced offense. After receiving the nod to replace Bill Kenney as the starting quarterback, the aging, but reliable Steve DeBerg sprayed passes to eight receivers, hitting 22 of 37 for 285 yards, with zero interceptions, and a TD pass to Stephone Paige that cut the lead to 21-16.

But things looked bleak when Stanford Jennings ran back the ensuing kickoff 98 yards to score.

After Lowery kicked his fourth field goal from 47 yards the score was 28-19 and holding as the fourth quarter dissolved. With 6:06 remaining Albert Lewis, who earlier had recovered a fumble to set up points, blocked a Bengals punt through the end zone for a safety. After the free kick the Chiefs drove to the Bengals' 1, and Christian Okoye plunged into the end zone. Lowery's point-after tied the score at 28 with 1:11 left.

Esiason knew before the game he would be up against the second-toughest secondary statistically in the league. The Chiefs limited the opposition to 158 passing yards per game heading into that contest, but were without cornerback Kevin Ross who was injured.

Deron Cherry, who was tied for second in the NFL with six interceptions at the time, came up with a huge steal that gave the Chiefs a final possession, and Lowery kicked one true from 39 yards with 00:02 on the clock. Cherry, linebacker Andy Hawkins and Jayice Pearson, who replaced the injured Ross, all had five tackles for the Chiefs. Carlos Carson caught seven passes for 86 yards, and Okoye gained 102 yards on 16 carries.

Peterson obviously liked what he saw, and the rest ... well, you know what they say about history.

Despite battling through a season slowed by injuries, Christian Okoye rushed for 102 yards against the Bengals. It included a 48-yard run, which was a career high at the time. (© Young Company)

Jayice Pearson, who signed with the Chiefs as a free agent midway through the '86 season, replaced the injured Kevin Ross against the Bengals, and contributed with five tackles. (© Young Company)

Deron Cherry celebrated after the interception that helped set up the winning field goal. (© Young Company)

A joyous occasion after kicking the winning field goal, Nick Lowery celebrates with rookie Neil Smith, (#90) who started seven games that year. One week later, Lowery kicked a 40-yard FG with 46 seconds left in the game to lift the Chiefs to a 27-24 victory over Seattle. Lowery missed only five of 32 FG attempts in '88. (© Young Company)

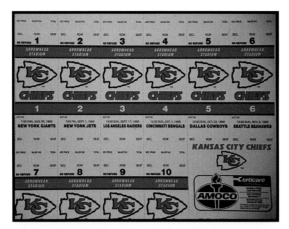

RAIDER HATER IV: SEPT. 17, 1989
Attendance: 71,741 Temp: 75
Chiefs 24, Raiders 19...DT's 1st sack, and more...O-Koy-yay, O-Kay...Martin miffed at Marcus.

"We may have something here," Lamar Hunt footnoted. "The first of many." A solid upending of the Darth Vaders started a trend under President/General Manager Carl Peterson and Coach Marty Schottenheimer like nothing the Chiefs had ever experienced—consistent dominance of the Black-and-Silver: 14 wins in the first 17 meetings, including eight straight over its most despised rival.

No. 1 draft pick Derrick Thomas, who recorded one tackle in his first game the week before at Denver, also started a trend that would become endearing to Chiefs fans: he plastered QB Jay Schroeder for the first of his eventual team record sacks, and finished the day with two sacks, five tackles, and a forced fumble. And the first of the Thomas-Neil Smith combo sacks went in the books, plus Smith recorded one of his own.

The rest of the defense queued up for honors, too. Kevin Ross intercepted a pass, Walker Lee Ashley and Rob McGovern made nine tackles each at linebacker, and Dan Saleaumua, whose emotional cup runneth over, matched Thomas's five.

Schottenheimer said of budding star Thomas, who became All-Pro from the get-go, "We are of the opinion that he will make plays that other guys won't. He is a young man loaded with talent." Thomas said his initial sack felt "just like my last one in college (at Alabama)...I loved the Raiders before the game started, and now I love that it's over."

The swarming 'D' held Marcus Allen to 58 yards on 18 carries. Chiefs LB Chris Martin got into brief fisticuffs with Allen. "The hype of the game made any little hit more than it actually was," Martin said. "I hit him and dragged him a little, and he wanted to scruff. We ironed things out by the end of the game. He told me not to worry about it."

Allen, who four years later would swap uniforms and don Chiefs red-and-gold, said simply, "This was like every other Chiefs game in Kansas City—

While opening a new regime at home under Coach Marty Schottenheimer, a past tradition was rekindled with the return of the Wolfpack section in Kansas City. (© Young Company)

rough." Nose tackle Billy Bob Maas got tossed for swinging at Raiders back Steven Wright.

Kansas City's offense had smoother sailing. Steve DeBerg had 12 for 18 passing accuracy, hitting Chris Dressel for a 49-yard touchdown and 7-6 temporary lead. Christian Okoye returned from five weeks off because of injury, and he bulled for 95 yards on 27 carries, two of which scored short-yardage touchdowns. The last one, with 7:51 left, brought the Chiefs from behind for the third time.

Schottenheimer sang praise to a viable force that had been missing from the Chiefs aresenal for many years—a nearly full house of fans. "Our fans certainly got their money's worth," he said. "Their presence is a very important part of what we're trying to do here. We appreciate that."

As a newcomer in Kansas City after two seasons in Detroit, Dan Saleaumua (#97) got acquainted with his teammates and with Raiders quarterback Jay Schroeder in the heat of the battle. (© Young Company)

Jonathan Hayes and Robb Thomas help usher in the Chiefs-Raiders rivalry under the new administration. (© Young Company)

MARTY'S REVENGE:
SEPT. 30, 1990
Attendance: 75,462
Temp: 68
Chiefs 34, Browns 0...Two Schotts rang out...So did two punts!

"Big Time!" That was Marty Schottenheimer's ringing endorsement of victory over his former team. Sharing the joyous occasion—six assistants from his old Browns staff, including his brother, Kurt in charge of special teams.

"Seldom has a group of coaches looked more satisfied," Lamar Hunt said. In their first face-off at Arrowhead since Schottenheimer departed Cleveland, where he loved them and they loved him, the Schotts & Co. didn't simply win. They cruised.

The year before, in their first meeting, at Cleveland the teams had tied 10-10, and Marty Schottenheimer had pulled out the old line about kissing your sister. This time he said, "It's like kissing your wife!"

The day was filled with big plays. Steve DeBerg passed to Robb Thomas on a 47-yard play that opened the scoring. Later, DeBerg found Emile Harry for a 6-yard touchdown. Nick Lowery kicked field goals of 39 and 34 yards. DeBerg enjoyed an efficient day—12 for 21, no intercepts, 189 yards, two TDs. Stephone Paige caught four for almost half the yardage, 90.

And to Kurt Schottenheimer's pleasure, his special teams blocked two punts. Charles Washington blocked one, and Martin ran it 31 yards for a TD. Albert Lewis blocked the other, just as he had at Green Bay the Sunday before, and Kevin Ross scooped it up and ran 4 yards for the TD that punctuated the rout.

Browns head coach Bud Carson, formerly a member of the Chiefs staff, groused in defeat, "It's a sad commentary on this coaching staff that a team like the Chiefs can block two kicks the previous week, and then block two against us. I've never been so sick about something in my life. That first block turned the game around."

Kick blocking became a trademark of this year's team. That, plus kick coverage and scoring led Kurt Schottenheimer to an award as the NFL's Special Teams co-Coach of the Year.

Paige said, "They had a good thing in Cleveland, and they let them go. We appreciate what we have here."

Before meeting the Browns, the Chiefs opened the 1990 season at home with a 24-21 win over the Minnesota Vikings. Do you recognize the Vikings player (#16) over Steve DeBerg's shoulder? Hint: He later played quarterback for the Chiefs and replaced Steve Bono as the starter at the end of the '96 season. (© Young Company)

Kevin Porter (#27) and Charles Washington (#46) each provided big plays for Kurt Schottenheimer's special teams with blocked punts. Added to Washington's blocked punt against the Cleveland Browns was one against Miami in the playoffs. Porter blocked a punt against the Raiders that set up a key field goal for the Chiefs. (© Young Company)

Only seven years earlier, Bud Carson worked as defensive coordinator for the Chiefs. He returned as the Browns Head Coach with the dubious honor of bringing most of the players Marty Schottenheimer knew well when the Browns played at Arrowhead. (© Young Company)

After playing six years as a nose tackle, Bill Maas was switched to defensive end in 1990, where he played while attending the University of Pittsburgh. Seen here battling in the trenches against the Browns, Maas finished with his best season sack total (5) since 1987. His finest game of the year was against Detroit, which earned him AFC Defensive Player of the Week honors.
(© Young Company)

Steve DeBerg hooked up with tight end Alfredo Roberts on a 37-yard pass that set up one of five Chiefs touchdowns on the day against Detroit. Roberts, an eighth round draft choice in 1988, played three seasons with the Chiefs. (© Young Company)

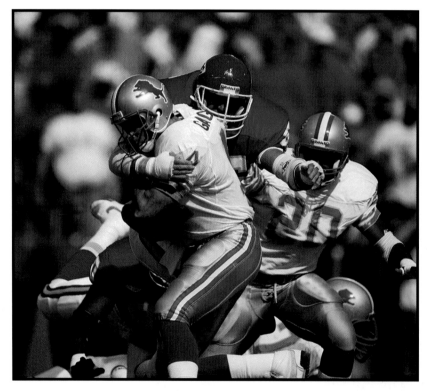

Lions quarterback Bob Gagliano, who played for the Chiefs from 1981-83, feels the heat from Chiefs linebacker Dino Hackett. While injuries shortened Hackett's career, he played in every game during the 1990 season. (© Young Company)

WORD PLAY:
OCT. 14, 1990
Attendance: 74,312
Temp: 66
Chiefs 43, Lions 24...425 yards of Barrys...Stat sheet bulges... Offensive line fine.

For a few fleeting seasons Barry Word provided the Chiefs with a heart-warming human interest story, and half of a battering-ram backfield tandem with Christian Okoye. Word, a standout at Virginia, had revived his career after off-field troubles. Word's finest day in the sun unfolded before a packed house who watched him surpass the club record for yards rushing in a game with 200 on 18 carries—all the sweeter with the famous Heisman Barry on the opposing side.

Barry Sanders was no slouch for Detroit, gaining 90 yards on 16 runs, plus 135 yards on five pass receptions. He and Word each scored two touchdowns. Word's pounding was complemented by Christian Okoye's 91 yards on 23 carries. The onslaught of offense by the teams mounted 894 yards and 67 points, one of the busiest days ever for the Arrowhead scoreboard operator. The Chiefs, gaining 566 yards, scored once by air, a 1-yarder from Steve DeBerg (15/26/256) to tight end Jonathan Hayes. DeBerg made several passes that set up ground scores—60 yards to Emile Harry, 46 to Todd McNair, and 37 to Alfredo Roberts.

Okoye ran in the go-ahead touchdown from 4 yards with 5:55 left in the first half, and another from the 1. Word scored on runs of 53 and 1. Nick Lowery kicked 21-and 32-yard field goals. The other two points came on a tackle for safety by Bill Maas, who also forced a fumble to go with his two sacks. Petry had an interception and Neil Smith recovered a fumble.

Sanders, who comes from Wichita, Kansas and played at Oklahoma State, thrilled the crowd by running out a 47-yard touchdown pass play from Bob Gagliano, and also scored a 13 yard rushing TD.

Special mention is appropriate for some usually unsung standouts:

Lewis Cooper on the kickoff coverage team made four tackles.

The Chiefs' starting offensive line, which can fairly be termed awesome during this era, came together primarily through the draft between

If Albert Lewis wasn't blocking punts, he was harassing the opposing punter, the Lions' Jim Arnold in this case, a former Chiefs teammate of Lewis. In 1990, Lewis blocked four punts en route to his fourth straight Pro Bowl berth. (© Young Company)

1983-'90. It comprised left tackle John Alt (No. 1 draftee in 1984 out of Iowa), left guard Dave Szott (7th round, 1990, Penn State), center Tim Grunhard (2nd round, 1990, Notre Dame), right guard David Lutz (2nd round, 1983, Georgia Tech), right tackle Rich Baldinger (free agent, 1983, Wake Forest), and tight end Jonathan Hayes (2nd round, 1985, Iowa).

Barry Word, who did not start a game in the NFL for three years, led the Chiefs in rushing with 1,015 yards in the 1990 season. (© Young Company)

Emile Harry's 60-yard catch against the Lions was the longest of his career at the time. (© Young Company)

Albert Lewis was named the AFC Defensive Player of the Week for his performance against the Raiders. Lewis intercepted a Jay Schroeder pass, deflected two others and recovered a fumble in that contest. (© Young Company)

RAIDER HATER V:
NOV. 4, 1990
Attendance: 70,951
Temp: 37, light rain
(wind chill 20)
Chiefs 9, Raiders 7...
Bo, meet Deron...

Deron Cherry can count many momentous plays, but none distinguishes him any more than his first play on a day charged with emotion. Raiders were the invaders—that's enough to stir the blood by itself. Add to it that Cherry was back in action after 10 months of rehabilitation of a knee injury, and Bo Jackson, he of the Royals' outfield, was on the football field for the first time following the end of the baseball season.

It couldn't have come at a better time to drop a Cherry bomb. His return from an injury that occurred the season before against San Diego coincided with a desperate chance to close in on the first place Raiders who were atop the AFC West with a 6-1 record, two games ahead of the 4-3 Chiefs. One would have to go back to the '73 season, the Chiefs' second year at Arrowhead, to find a Chiefs-Raiders battle this late in the year when the two teams were in 1-2 positions.

They collided on one of the most memorable single plays in Arrowhead history:

Bo carried. Cherry met him head-on. The jarring tackle sent the ball flying free of Jackson's grip. The Chiefs recovered, turned it into a score, and pressed on to a tense victory.

Cherry recalled, "I was one of the first guys in the locker room before the game and I met (safety) Kevin Porter in the training room. And he said, 'I had a dream about you.'" After Porter hesitated on revealing his dream, Cherry pressed him. "He said, 'On your first play you hit the running back and he fumbled.' I said, 'Yeah, right' and went my merry way."

The play happened in the second quarter when both Cherry and Jackson made their first appearances. Cherry described the shot heard 'round Arrowhead:

"They lined up in the I (formation). In studying film, I knew their tendency was 100 percent run. So I thought, 'I'm not going to drop (back),' and I cheated up a little bit. In lining up from their own end zone, I see a hole open up and I see our

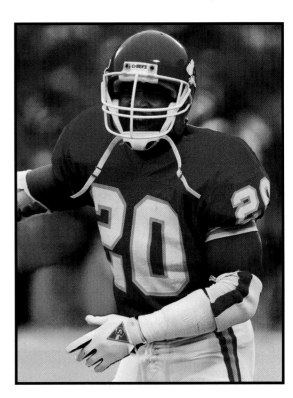

Deron Cherry is remembered for the Bo Jackson hit. (photo by Tim Umphrey)

linebacker get blocked.

"Now it's me and him. I'm thinking what am I going to do? Stop him or hit him? If I just try to cut him, he's going all the way. So I wound up and laid into him. I put my helmet on the ball and the next thing I heard is the crowd noise. I got up and turned and the first person I saw was K.P. (Porter). I high-fived him, and the look in his eyes was like he had just seen a ghost."

The crowd was on edge to the finish, after Nick Lowery had provided a two-point lead on a 41-yard field goal. The Chiefs still had to make it hold up another 12 minutes.

Neither side generated much offense in the biting, wet conditions. Jackson (40) and Marcus Allen (24) mustered just 64 Raider yards on a combined 17 carries. Barry Word gained 85 on 15 carries for the Chiefs. Lowery had provided a 6-0 halftime lead with field goals of 36 and 48 yards. Steve Smith put the Raiders ahead with a touchdown on the first play of the fourth quarter.

The Chiefs relied mainly on defense to seal this tight one, thriving on an interception by Albert Lewis, two fumble recoveries (Lewis and Pearson), and Porter's blocked punt. Derrick Thomas had a sack, and Dan Saleaumua led the team with six tackles.

NO DOUBTING THOMAS AS SACK-KING (7): NOV. 11, 1990

Attendance: 71,285
Temp: 63

Seahawks 17, Chiefs 16...Last-play lament...Derrick's deluge dumps Dave on derriere.

This ranks as probably the most memorable regular season loss on the floor of Arrowhead, given the soaring wave of emotions over Derrick Thomas' unbelievable day in the Seattle backfield. The wave came crashing down with stunning force when what appeared momentarily to be his eighth sack—and fourth in the desperate, clinging, closing minutes—eluded his grasp, and turned instead into defeat on the last play of the game.

Whooooo. It leaves you breathless just to remember it.

Dave Krieg, was the stun gun, escaping what seemed certain to be Thomas's final thrust into his team's heart, and throwing a victorious touchdown pass as the clock wound down to zero-zero-zero-zero.

"That's the loudest crowd in the NFL, but at that particular time, it was the quietest crowd when Paul Skansi caught the pass," Krieg said.

His feat was all the more amazing because he had spent much of the afternoon buried beneath the body of the Chiefs' perennial All-Pro linebacker. Thomas put Krieg on his duff seven times for an NFL record that accumulated 60 yards in losses for the Seahawks.

Thomas' pursuit even prevented Krieg from knowing, that the final pass had been completed, until the crowd fell silent. "I didn't even see him catch it because Mr. Thomas had chased me all around and I think I finally wore him out because he couldn't finish the sack and I was able to get away from him."

The game see-sawed into the climactic final moments on the running of Christian Okoye (21 carries, 85 yards) and passing of Steve DeBerg (16/30/124), mostly to Robb Thomas (7/53), for the Chiefs, and the finely-tuned passing of Krieg (16/23/306, two touchdowns) for Seattle. Krieg used eight different receivers, including Skansi for 25 yards on the fateful last play. Johnson kicked the extra point that won it.

When Krieg and Skansi, who is in the college

Robb Thomas caught a career high seven passes against the Seattle Seahawks, a team for whom he later played, but ended up a forgotten accomplishment in light of the final result. (© Young Company)

While Dave Krieg felt the heat from the Chiefs defense, David Lutz (#72) and the rest of the Chiefs offensive line kept Steve DeBerg protected enough to endure 22 sacks on the year, the fourth-fewest in the NFL. (© Young Company)

coaching business, hook up on the golf course, that game usually pops up in conversation.

"We have great memories of that because of how we worked to get one win there," said Krieg who steered the Seahawks to the win after eight straight losses at Arrowhead.

Dan Saleaumua had given the Chiefs a 16-10 lead near the end of the third quarter with a fumble recovery in the end zone. Kevin Ross caused the fumble. Nick Lowery's field goals of 25, 30 and 24 put the earlier points on the board. Besides Thomas, Chris Martin and Smith had sacks, too, and Martin recovered a fumble.

With the game safely tucked away, Marty Schottenheimer received a Monday Night Gatorade bath.

A SPECTACLE: MNF, LEVY'S BILLS, AND VICTORY! OCT. 7, 1991
Attendance: 76,120
Temp: 70
Chiefs 33, Bills 6... Lowery, Thomas give 'em, what?—four... Double trouble backfield... Tailgate heaven.

The night held a magical quality.

Frank and Al and Dan, the Monday Night Football crew, revisited for the first time in eight years. Coach Marv Levy was back in town as the Buffalo Bills revisited for the first time in five years. The Bills were 5-0, the AFC's only unbeaten team, while the Chiefs were riding a two-game winning streak. The parking lot filled early, the tailgate smoke wafted high (causing the MNF crew to drool and rave on the air), and 76,120 turned out

when they could have stayed home and watched it on TV. Only the Dallas Cowboys had drawn more fans in the first 19 home games of the Peterson-Schottenheimer era.

"That was a special feeling, that whole day," Bill Maas said. "When you pulled into the parking lot-we got there as players four hours ahead of time-there was already electricity in the parking lot. You knew that that was a special day when we walked into that stadium. There was something different about that game and everybody could feel it, all the fans, the players. Everybody knew it."

Before the kickoff, Pack Band bandleader Tony DiPardo never experienced the singing of the Star-Spangled Banner like he did that night, "I heard a choir of 76,000 voices singing the Anthem. The ambience was incredible. They set off fireworks during the player introductions," he said.

Derrick studies the opponents from Buffalo. (photo by Chris Dennis)

The Chiefs responded to the combined elements in fine fettle, completely dominating the defending AFC champions, 33-6. Nick Lowery kicked four field goals, and Derrick Thomas made four sacks. Christian Okoye and Harvey Williams moved the ball 233 yards on the ground, and Steve DeBerg passed for 150.

Lowery set the tone just 2 minutes into the game with a 41-yard field goal, and the Chiefs dominated from there. Later he was good from 40, 24 and 22 yards on a perfect 4-for-4 night. Okoye carried 29 times for 130 yards and two touchdowns, 5 and 2 yarders. Williams gained 103 on 20 carries. DeBerg was sharp, mostly short, hitting 16 of his 23 attempts, and one to Pete Holohan scored a touchdown from the 1. Robb Thomas caught four passes for 55 yards.

Maas added two sacks to Thomas's four, leaving Jim Kelly on his back or scrambling all night under the rush.

"It was ALL Chiefs. Offense. Defense. All cylinders were hitting for us," Maas said. "It was really a

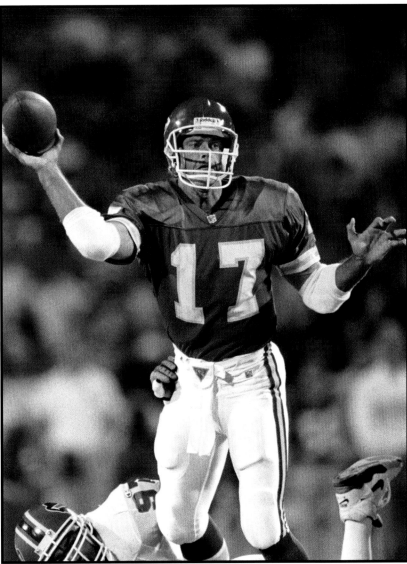

Quarterback Steve DeBerg was on target while the Chiefs offense clicked. He missed on only 7 of 23 pass attempts (© Young Company)

step up for us as a team. I think the nation was amused. I think the nation saw that Kansas City is back, back to where it once was in its glory days in the early 70s."

The setting, the results, the nation looking in— all the qualities of this autumnal spectacle created one of the biggest rushes ever experienced by folks in the seats at Arrowhead. The Chiefs used it as a springboard to another smashing victory over the Miami Dolphins (revenge for the heartbreaking playoff loss that ended the previous season), extending the winning streak to four and pushing toward the playoffs again.

RAIDER HATER VI— HANKERIN' FOR SOME FOOTBALL: OCT. 28, 1991
Attendance: 77,111
Temp: 68
Chiefs 24, Raiders 21... Three minutes of gloom... Certain doom... 'Til Burruss goes vrooom.

In his last season with the Chiefs, Lloyd Burruss (#34), came up with the biggest play of his career against the Raiders. Three days shy of his 34th birthday, Burruss returned an interception 83 yards to set up the winning touchdown.
(© Young Company)

The winning streak ended at four in Denver by a hair, 19-16, but Kansas City fans were not disheartened. They could recharge on their emotions with the Raiders coming to town, and for all the world to see. They were ready for some bloodball, as, so soon after so long an absence, Monday Night pageantry enveloped Arrowhead again, just three weeks removed from their previous visit.

Buffalo was a tough act to follow, but this classic rivalry developed yet another dramatic script. The Chiefs rallied from behind, and scored the game-winner late after a spectacular interception runback by Lloyd Burruss.

An overflow crowd— largest in 20 seasons at Arrowhead, largest of the new regime's first 28 home dates (counting preseason), and foretelling of what to expect for many years to come—put the Chiefs before more than 305,000 fans in their four games of October.

The Raiders stunned them into silence in the middle of the first quarter, taking an 11-0 lead in three minutes, 13 seconds of lightning strikes. Ahead 21-10, the Raiders drove in the fourth quarter toward what everybody felt was about to be a stake-in-the-heart score when Lloyd Burruss caused the lulled crowd to erupt. He intercepted a pass, ran it 83 yards for a touchdown setup—a play that propelled the Chiefs from doom into a 14-point fourth-quarter turnaround that stole victory. "Goose bumps!" Lamar Hunt declared.

As Burruss gasped for air on the sideline, Steve DeBerg fired to Tim Barnett in the end zone from the 6-yard line to complete the dramatic comeback with just 47 ticks left on the clock. DeBerg had started the engine just before halftime with an 8-yard

strike to Bill Jones, dipping into L. A.'s 18-0 lead.

The Raiders struck in the fifth minute of the game; Greg Townsend returned an interception 31 yards to the Chiefs' 1. The Chiefs would reflect later on how monumental a goal line stand was way back in that opening sequence. Tackles by Dino Hackett, Albert Lewis and Tracey Simien forced the Raiders to settle for an 18-yard Jaeger field goal. They struck again just 1:43 later when Torin Dorn tackled Barnett for a safety, and 1:30 after the free kick Ricky Bell plunged from the 1, where a 59-yard pass play from Jay Schroeder to Mervyn Fernandez ended.

The safety was one of the wildest plays ever witnessed at Arrowhead. On third down at the L-A 18, DeBerg fumbled. Aaron Wallace seemed to have it, bound for a Raiders touchdown at the five, but the ball squirted free again and Barnett scrambled for possession, falling on it at the goal line as Dorn fell on him. Again, the Chiefs were spared six. So, between the defensive stand and the safety, they trailed 5-0 instead of 14-0—a large difference 54 minutes later.

The teams traded field goals in the third period, Nick Lowery hitting from 33 to make the score 21-10. And then the drama unfolded. The Raiders drove toward the Chiefs' goal line in the fourth minute of the fourth quarter, 3rd-and-goal at the 6. Burruss stepped in front of a Jay Schroeder pass at the 2, ran until he turned into butter at the Raiders' 15, and the Chiefs pounded it in from there—Christian Okoye scoring from the 1 with about half a quarter left.

That time was fleeting when Bill Maas made a huge sack and the Raiders had to punt. The Chiefs had good field position—their 43—but faltered with a penalty. And then everybody held their breath during a playback review—remember those?—of a DeBerg-to-Robb Thomas pass. The 8-yard gain just after the two-minute warning stood, DeBerg continued to spread passes around (he used eight receivers this night, Barnett gathering five for 45 yards), until the connection with Barnett that started with 0:51 remaining.

Okoye (62) and Harvey Williams (53) gained steady yardage to complement DeBerg's spraygun effect in the air. But the defense provided the cornerstone for this thriller. Jayice Pearson and Deron Cherry also had interceptions, and Derrick Thomas, Neil Smith and Chris Martin provided sacks.

Another victory over the Raiders in the last game of the season in Los Angeles set up yet a third meeting, the following week—the first playoff game ever at Arrowhead . . . .

RAIDER HATER VII— THE PLAYOFFS COME TO TOWN: DEC. 28, 1991
Attendance: 75,827
Temp: 38, overcast, fog
Chiefs 10, Raiders 6... Cherry very busy... Thomas, too, as 'D' reigns supreme.

It took a generation of Chiefs fans, 20 seasons, for the playoffs to land in Arrowhead. A swelling crowd braved the dank elements among 77, 791 ticketholders to soak in the atmosphere (1, 964 no-shows). What could be better, or more appropriate, than for the most intense of the Chiefs' rivals to bear the brunt of the long wait. Welcome to Kansas City, Mssrs. Davis, Allen, Gault, Marinovich (Schroeder was hurt), Long, Golic, Townsend, and the Lott of you nasty foes.

Not only was the home playoff game a new experience to many of the Chiefs players, but also to the fans and the stadium personnel. Stadium Announcer Dan Roberts, in particular, felt butterflies before that contest, which makes that game most memorable to him, "I was a little tense that day and I was happy at the same time because it was a new experience."

Deron Cherry continued to big-play his way toward eventual Chiefs Hall of Fame status with two interceptions in the bitter cold of pre-noon during Christmas week, running his career total to 50. He made a 29-yard runback on one, 17 on the other. Cherry also led the team in tackles with seven solo and an assist. Nobody else had more than four.

As halftime approached in a scoreless battle, the Raiders threatened. On 3rd-and-16 at the Chiefs' 32, Todd Marinovich threw a pass and Chiefs corner-

back Eric Everett picked it off at the KC 11 and returned it 23 yards. The Chiefs took control, clung to it desperately and barely, but never relinquished the lead that a Steve DeBerg-to-Fred Jones pass (11 yards) and Nick Lowery's PAT created 5:07 before the half.

Jeff Jaeger kicked a pair of field goals, 32 and 26 yards, the first just 21 seconds before halftime and the other late in the third period as the Raiders closed to 7-6. Nick Lowery, who had missed wide left from 33 and short from 47 earlier in the game, expanded the lead early in the fourth period with an 18-yard chip shot.

The Raiders then self-destructed during a possible go-ahead drive in the final 4 minutes, taking four penalties for 40 yards. A biggie occurred during a 28-yard pass to the Chiefs' 24: Ethan Horton, a former No. 1 draft pick by the Chiefs as a running back, playing tight end for the Raiders, was caught holding. The Raiders wound up back at their own 41—just one yard ahead of where they started.

On the next play Lonnie Marts intercepted Marinovich at the KC 47, returned it seven yards, and the Chiefs killed the clock.

Barry Word was the drive shaft for the Chiefs' offense. He ran 33 times, gained 130 yards, and spun the longest gain of the day, 23. The other cogs in the Chiefs' threesome of rushing threats, Harvey Williams, another top draft choice who would later wind up in a Raiders suit, and Christian Okoye carried but three times between them.

Steve DeBerg passed sparingly, completing 9 of 14 for 89 yards among five receivers—Robb Thomas

Nick Lowery kicked a field goal beyond the reach of the Raider defenders, which put the game out of reach and safely in the Chiefs' hands (© Young Company)

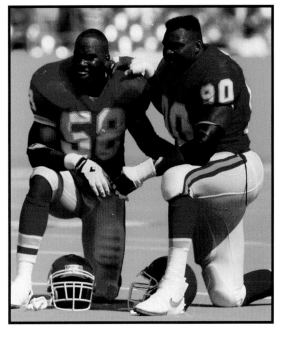

A quarterback's worst nightmare, Derrick Thomas and Neil Smith. (photo by Tim Umphrey)

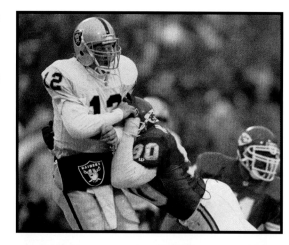

Todd Marinovich probably wished he would have stayed at USC for all four years instead of turning pro early after some of the hits he absorbed against the Chiefs, like this one from Neil Smith. (© Young Company)

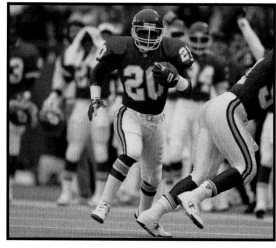

Deron Cherry, seen here returning one of his two interceptions, went out in a blaze of glory in his last game at Arrowhead Stadium (© Young Company)

THE 1991 PLAYOFFS

THE CHIEFS' STARTING LINEUPS

Offense

SE   Robb Thomas, Oregon State
LT   John Alt, Iowa
LG   Dave Szott, Penn State
C   Tim Grunhard, Notre Dame
RG   David Lutz, Georgia Tech
RT   Derrick Graham, Appalachian St.
TE   Jonathan Hayes, Iowa
FL   Emile Harry, Stanford
QB   Steve DeBerg, San Jose State
RB   Barry Word, Virginia
RB   Bill Jones, SW Texas State

Defense

LE   Neil Smith, Nebraska
NT   Dan Saleaumua, Arizona State
RE   Bill Maas, Pitt
LOLB   Chris Martin, Auburn
LILB Tracy Simien, Texas Christian
RILB Dino Hackett, Appalachian St.
ROLB   Derrick Thomas, Alabama
LC   Jayice Pearson, Washington
RC   Kevin Ross, Temple
SS   Kevin Porter, Auburn
FS   Deron Cherry, Rutgers
PK   Nick Lowery, Dartmouth
P   Bryan Barker, Santa Clara

Substitutes

RB James Saxon, San Jose State...RB/KR Troy Stradford, Boston College...S Lloyd Burruss, Maryland...RB Christian Okoye, Azusa Pacific...CB Eric Everett, Texas Tech...CB Anthony Parker, Arizona State...S Charles Mincy, Washington...RB Harvey Williams, LSU...RB Todd McNair, Temple...OLB Lonnie Marts, Tulane...LB Tracy Rogers, Fresno State...LB Ervin Randle, Baylor...G Frank Winters, Western Illinois...T Rich Baldinger, Wake Forest...WR Fred Jones, Grambling...WR Tim Barnett, Jackson State...WR J.J. Birden, Oregon...TE Pete Holohan, Notre Dame...NT Tom Sims, Pitt...DE Leonard Griffin, Grambling. (Did Not Play: QB Mark Vlasic, Iowa. Not Active: QB Steve Pelluer,

Washington...T Joe Valerio, Penn.)

THE RAIDERS' STARTING LINEUPS

Offense

WR:Willie Gault, LT: Bruce Wilkerson, LG: Steve Wisniewski, C: Don Mosebar, RG: Max Montoya, RT: Steven Wright, TE: Ethan Horton, WR: Mervyn Fernandez, QB: Todd Marinovich, RB: Steve Smith, RB: Marcus Allen.

Defense

LE: Howie Long, LT: Bob Golic, RT: Scott Davis, RE: Greg Townsend, LLB: Winston Moss, MLB: Riki Ellison, RLB: Aaron Wallace, LCB: Terry McDaniel, RCB: Lionel Washington, SS: Ronnie Lott, FS: Eddie Anderson.

P: Jeff Gossett

PK: Jeff Jaeger.

Substitutes

S: Derrick Crudup, S: Dan Land, RB: Nick Bell, RB: Napoleon McCallum, S: Elvis Patterson, CB: Torin Dorn, LB: Mike Jones, LB: Tom Benson, LB: Jerry Robinson, DT: Roy Hart, C: Dan Turk, T: J Fitzpatrick, DT: Nolan Harrison, T: Reggie McElroy, WR: Tim Brown, WR: Jamie Holland, WR: Sam Graddy, TE: Andrew Glover, DE: Anthony Smith. (Did not play: QB Jay Schroeder, RB Roger Craig. Not active: QB Vince Evans, CB Tahaan Lewis.)

The Officials

Referee	Jerry Markbreit
Umpire	Dave Hamilton
Line Judge	John Alderton
Side Judge	Mike Carey
Head Linesman	Ron Phares
Back Judge	Bob Moore
Field Judge	Don Orr
Replay Official	Mike Kamanski

(3), Bill Jones and Fred Jones (2 each), J.J. Birden and Barry Word, who added eight yards to his day with a reception.

Bryan Barker's punting also was significant for the Chiefs. He kicked just two, and averaged 46 yards for excellent field position. In contrast Raiders punter Jeff Gossett had only one kick, and it fluttered 20 yards.

Others who were in on the most tackles for the Chiefs included Derrick Thomas and Chris Martin, each with a sack for minus-8 yards; Dan Saleaumua, Ervin Randle, Jayice Pearson, and Neil Smith. Saleaumua and Bill Maas recovered Raiders fumbles caused by Thomas and Marts.

Raiders who kept their team in contention included running back Nick Bell (20/107), quarterback Todd Marinovich (12/23/140/4 interceptions), tight end Ethan Horton (3/59), wide receiver Tim Brown (4/45), safety Ronnie Lott (interception, 4 tackles), defensive tackle Steve Davis (5 tackles, 2 sacks for minus-16), defensive tackle Bob Golic (7 tackles), and defensive end Greg Townsend (6 tackles).

Notably, Marcus Allen carried just seven times for 39 yards (in another two seasons he would begin to enjoy the fruits of Arrowhead support in record-setting performances for the Chiefs). WR Willie Gault, a world-class sprinter who was always dangerous on pass routes, caught just one for 11 yards.

The Chiefs rode the wave of anticipation and excitement and victory into the second round of playoffs. The season ended abruptly on frozen tundra in Buffalo, as the Bills returned the earlier spanking, 37-14. At season's end Cherry retired.

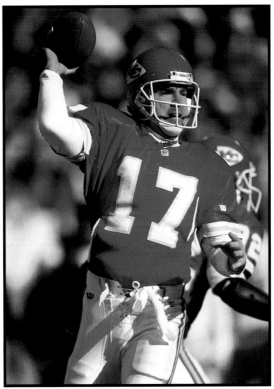

FLYING WITH (AND OVER) THE EAGLES:
OCT. 11, 1992
Attendance: 76,626
Temp: 59
Chiefs 24, Eagles 17...' Family' losses cast pall... Krieg's on OUR side now.

David Krieg—remember he of the dastardly deed two years previously?!—gave the Chiefs a sorely-needed injection of go-juice. The team had endured a troubled summer of two deaths in the family—director of player personnel Whitey Dovell, and Hall of Fame lineman Buck Buchanan—and the retirement of six-time Pro Bowl safety Deron Cherry.

The Eagles swooped into town undefeated (5-0), while Schottenheimer's troops were reeling with injuries and self-doubt (3-2). "It was a big game for us because we didn't want to drop to .500," said Krieg, who was in his first season as starter for the Chiefs at quarterback after signing as a Plan B free agent. His previous 12 years in the NFL were spent in Seattle.

"Playing in the Kingdome earlier, I thought that was a great crowd, but the Arrowhead crowd was just amazing," Krieg said. "The fans there really helped our football team. I think the whole team enjoyed playing in front of the Arrowhead crowd."

Krieg's passing built a 24-3 lead in front of those who basked in a gloriously sunny setting. Krieg went deep (43 yards) and medium-deep (24 yards) on scoring plays with J. J. Birden, both in the first quarter, and really-deep to Willie Davis (74 yards) in the third quarter. Nick Lowery topped off the

day with a 20-yard field goal.

"We knew that we had the tendency to try to be a football team that ran the football, but we came out and surprised them with a lot of straight drop-backs. And a lot of play action passes where their safeties would come up and we were able to hit them for deep passes down the field," said Krieg.

Defensive gems held Philadelphia's hosses, such as Randall Cunningham and Keith Byars, at bay, and as good as Reggie White is, he couldn't do it alone on the Eagles defense as he was neutralized by the superb blocking of tackle Rich Baldinger.

Throughout that game, we had excellent protection from our offensive line," Krieg said, that protection held up so well he was the only quarterback in the NFL to throw all of his team's passes that year. "A defensive line as good as the Eagles can be intimidating, but I think with my two years with the Chiefs, and especially my first year, it was an offensive line that played well together and they battled."

Derrick Thomas registered three sacks, Neil Smith two, and Kevin Ross one. Lonnie Marts claimed a fumble, and Albert Lewis and Dale Carter gave the Chiefs two picks off of Cunningham. This day provided a great morale booster, but it faded quickly into a three-week funk . . . .

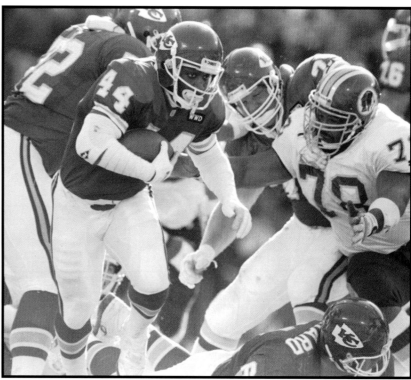

Rich Baldinger faced perhaps the biggest assignment of his career when he was tabbed to keep Philadelphia defensive end Reggie White off Dave Krieg's back. His play was an inspiration to his teammates. (© Young Company)

Against the Redskins, Harvey Williams rushed for a season-high 88 yards, but the Chiefs' number one draft choice of a year earlier had trouble breaking into a backfield that contained Christian Okoye and Barry Word, two 1,000-yard rushers. (© Young Company)

J.J. Birden enjoyed his finest season with the Chiefs in '92. His speed allowed him to become a legitimate deep threat. (© Young Company)

THE SKINS GAME: NOV. 15, 1992
Attendance: 75,238
Temp: 52
Chiefs 35, Redskins 16... A feast of Birden... Krieg tosses for 300

Two losses had followed the Eagles lift, and San Diego almost made it three in a row that would have sunk the Chiefs below .500 for one of the few times under Schottenheimer (and never this late in the season). With three more road games lying directly ahead, the Chiefs had to get well on the Washingtonians.

So be it. The Redskins came in 6-3, and left reeling by a 35-16 count. The Chiefs amazed their onlookers at Arrowhead with a thoroughly dominating defense in a 28-0 first half as Krieg, Christian Okoye, Harvey Williams and J.J. Birden paved the way on offense.

BRONC BUSTIN' GETS CHIEFS IN: DEC. 27, 1992
Attendance: 76,240
Temp: 45

Chiefs 42, Broncos 20... No-way Elway... The dee scores three... Carter cavorts.

A nemesis forever, John Elway and the Broncos, ventured into town with a chance to topple the Chiefs from a wild-card spot in the playoffs by tiebreaker, given an earlier 10-9 victory in Denver. Elway found no way. Actually, the Broncos did find a pair of touchdowns on his wing, and kicked a pair of field goals.

However, the Chiefs' defense left nothing to the imagination in this quest, smothering Elway with six sacks and scoring half of the Chiefs' touchdowns. Safety Charles Mincy, enjoying his only year as a starter, took a lateral from Bennie Thompson, who had intercepted Elway, and ran 32 yards for the first touchdown.

Rookie sensation Dale Carter, the No. 1 draft choice from Tennessee, returned an interception 36 yards for a touchdown and he also made a long punt return that set up another score.

As was the case so often over the years, Derrick Thomas thrived behind enemy lines. He sacked Elway three times, including once in the end zone in the fourth quarter. He jarred the ball loose from Denver's star, and fell on it for the final TD by the 'D.' Dave Krieg passed for two touchdowns.

Even though the exit would be quick at San Diego the next week, the Chiefs were in the playoffs for the third season in a string of six in a row.

Jonathan Hayes, a starter at tight end in all 16 games in 1992, was primarily a blocker, but had a career day in pass receptions against the Broncos. To help the Chiefs clinch a playoff berth, Hayes caught four passes for 44 yards and two touchdowns.
(© Young Company)

Derrick Thomas and John Elway have not had pleasant meetings when the Chiefs linebacker reaches the Broncos backfield. (Umphrey photo)

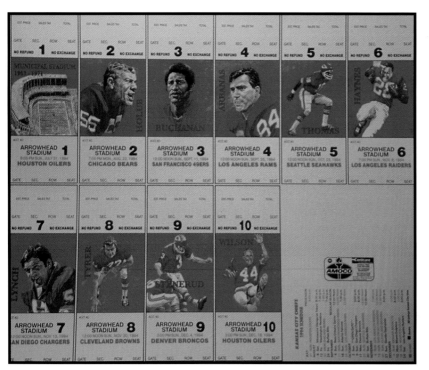

PLAYOFFS REDUX: JOE AND NICK RE-DO: JAN. 8, 1994
Attendance: 74,515
Temp: 25 (wind chill 18)
Chiefs 27, Steelers 24 (ot)... Chiefs 'Cash' in... Steelers unable to keep up with Jones

The sub-freezing climes kept a few faithful at home, yet an unbelievable band of merry followers cast bravado to the wind in order to witness Joe Montana, wearing rubber gloves for insulation, challenge the Steelers' notable wall of defense. Montana couldn't get a feel with the gloves, so he ditched them quickly. He rallied the Chiefs to a 24-all tie in the closing minutes after Keith Cash and Fred Jones made a momentous play.

Cash blocked a punt, and Jones ran it deep into Pittsburgh territory. Montana found Tim Barnett on fourth down for the touchdown with plenty of time left. Nick Lowery kicked the tying extra point, and had a chance to win it with a field goal before time ran out, but missed. He was true in overtime, though, and the Chiefs moved on to Houston for round two. "I remember saying to

Barnett at the locker next to mine, 'Were you worried on that fourth down play?'" Lowery said. "He said, 'Oh, was it fourth down?'"

Pittsburgh took a 7-0 lead when Neil O'Donnell connected with Adrian Cooper on a 10-yard pass, the first of O'Donnell's three TD tosses. He later hit Miller from 26 and Eric Green from 22, building a 24-17 lead and make things tense in the finishing minutes.

The Chiefs tied it once at 7-7 without Montana, who left the game temporarily because he was dizzy from a blindside hit as he threw. Dave Krieg subbed and connected with J. J. Birden for a 23-yard score. Lowery's first field goal, a 23-yarder, and a trademark Marcus Allen dive for a touchdown pulled the Chiefs into a tie again in a flurry of fourth-quarter activity that saw four scores and a missed field goal opportunity to win—all in the final nine minutes.

O'Donnell struck again with 4:11 left. Down 24-17, Montana brought the Chiefs back again, finding Barnett on the fourth-down thrill from the 7 with 1:43 left, capitalizing on the punt coverage team's monster play. Pittsburgh had lined up in punt formation at its own 48, nearly certain to bury the Chiefs in poor field position at the two-minute warning. Cash broke through, swatted the kick, and Jones picked it up at the 40. He made it to the Steelers' 9-yard line, and the offense handled it from there.

The defense held and provided one more opportunity. After four Montana passes, Lowery lined up 43 yards away, but pulled the kick wide with 12 seconds remaining. He found a reprieve in overtime. Montana took the Chiefs on a methodical 66-yard joyride on 11 plays that ate up six minutes. Completions to Cash for 18 and Birden for 10 put Lowery in easy range. He kicked the winner 32 yards with 3:57 on the clock.

D. J. Johnson of the Steelers got ejected from the game for a hit he put on Marcus Allen for a loss.

The Chiefs moved on and won in the Astrodome over the Oilers, but again had the season fizzle in Buffalo with a 30-13 thrashing in the AFC championship game.

JOE VS. THE 'NINERS: SEPT. 11, 1994
Attendance: 79,907
Temp: 83

Chiefs 24, 49ers 17... Chiefs strike (red and) gold... Montana no ordinary Joe... Young and the restless

If ever 80,000 were going to squeeze into Arrowhead again, this was the day for it.

In perhaps the most memorable of all games staged at Arrowhead in its first quarter-century, because of the buildup surrounding Joe Montana's first (and only) game against the team and teammates with whom he had created a mini-dynasty, the stands bulged. (Probably as time wears on, 800,000 will claim to have been there, for it was the place to be in the all-too-brief Peterson-Schottenheimer-Montana interlude of 1993-94.)

"It really wasn't that big a deal," Montana said in looking back, taking his usual low-keyed stance. Joe, it really was that big a deal. His former coach, George Seifert, acknowledged that after the game, "Obviously, this is one of the more publicized (games) and one that stands out a great deal because of all that Joe's done over the years, all the great things he's done. But, at the same time, when you get into the game, the game is the important thing."

Lamar Hunt labels it "the game of the century." The media crunch was astounding for a regular-season game, especially for so early in the season—just the second game—and Kansas City may never experience anything like it again. Writers even came from China for this one. Yes, China.

The perfect afternoon draped heat across the storied setting. The game didn't disappoint. Drama pervaded every stage of the three-hour struggle. Derrick Thomas made one of the plays that sticks in the memory, a sack of Steve Young in the end zone for a safety—one of three sacks by Thomas, who didn't find it easy tracking down the mobile Young.

"You know we got a lot of mobility over on defense. We got guys that can really pursue. We

Joe Montana spent 14 years with the 49ers before facing them in his second year with the Chiefs. (© Young Company)

Joe Valerio jolted the 49ers defense with a touchdown grab to open the scoring at the 5:44 mark of the first quarter. (© Young Company)

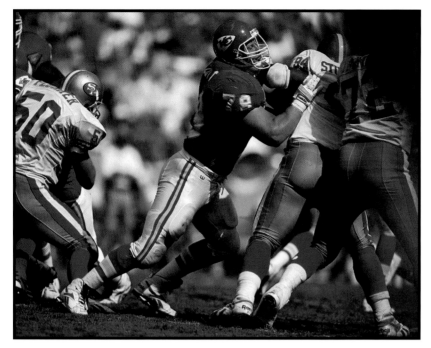

Chiefs guard David Szott, a seventh round draft choice out of Penn State, battled against former University of Kansas standout Dana Stubblefield in the trenches. (© Young Company)

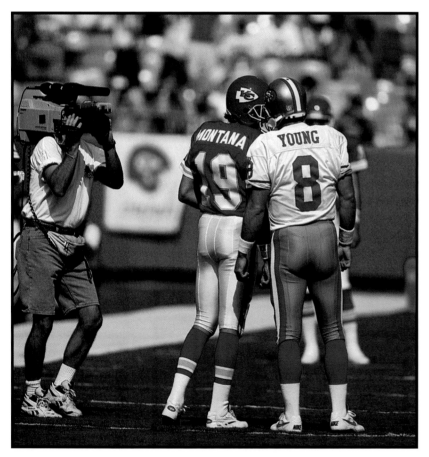

Joe Montana and Steve Young exchange pleasantries before the big showdown. (© Young Company)

just ran and ran and ran and kept running. I mean, that's the only way you defense that guy," said Thomas after the game.

Montana enjoyed a productive afternoon, completing 19 of 31 passes without an interception. He used seven receivers and accumulated 203 yards and two touchdowns. Keith Cash caught one scoring pass.

Scoring opened on a rare play that became a trademark of offensive tackle Joe Valerio. He lined up in the Chiefs' "tank" formation as tight end at the 49ers' 1-yard line, and Montana found him free for a touchdown. Valerio, a tall (6'-5") and hulking (295 lb.) target, scored on three touchdown passes during Montana's stint with the Chiefs and a fourth from Steve Bono in 1995.

Kimble Anders caught seven passes out of the backfield against the 49ers, and Willie Davis hauled in four for 59 yards. Marcus Allen, who gained 69 yards on 20 carries, shoved the other touchdown across from 4 yards out.

Though reluctant to talk about his first meeting against his old team, the Raiders, Allen spoke eagerly about Montana's encounter, "The 49ers game was exceptional, in anticipation of the matchup of Joe Montana and his successor, Steve Young."

Young, who helped San Francisco's run to the Super Bowl, also was sharp. He hit 24 of 34 for 288 yards, and Jerry Rice, as good a receiver as ever set foot on Arrowhead turf, caught five for 78 yards.

"I learned from the master and I've done it a number of times," said the downtrodden Young from the visiting locker room that day. "This would have been a really good time to do it (win), but it wasn't to be. I was excited about the opportunity."

Even though the 49ers put together 381 yards of offense (to KC's 292), the Chiefs' defense became staunch whenever it was needed—four sacks (Mark Collins added one to Thomas's count), two fumble recoveries (Jaime Fields and Jay Taylor). George Jamison made 10 tackles, Mark Collins and Tracy Rogers seven each, and Dale Carter six.

"It was a zoo," Chiefs public relations director Bob Moore said, "but it was a lot of fun. You'll probably never see anything like it again."

RAIDER HATER VIII—HALLELUJAH!
SEPT. 17, 1995
Attendance: 78,696
Temp: 71

Chiefs 23, Raiders 17... Brown reffed to the ground... Beaten with a Hasty retreat... A Schottenheimer smooch.

Always noteworthy, the Raiders rivalry provides a multitude of memorable freeze-frames. None is any more for the ages than when the "Hallelujah Corner," as dubbed by Chiefs safety William White (also referred to as "Amen Corner" by some), was visited on a freaky play that won the game for the Chiefs in overtime.

Tim Brown appeared to be open on a pass route that could have put the Raiders into field-goal range. But he ran into the umpire, Jeff Rice. James Hasty stepped into the breach, caught the Jeff Hostetler pass, and ran it back 64 yards for a touchdown, outrunning Hostetler and Napoleon Kaufman for the final thrust.

"I just wanted to get into the end zone," said Hasty after the game. "I didn't want to get shoved out of bounds."

He flopped to earth in the end zone as teammates scrambled wildly into a pile on top of him. (At first trainer Dave Kendall thought Hasty had pulled a muscle, by the way he fell, but it turned out that the cornerback was simply out of breath.)

Incredibly, two other game-breaker plays ended up in the same, southwest area of the end zone during the season, so Hasty suggested that the area should have a name. Somebody came up with "Amen Corner," but White rejected that because golf already claims it (an area at Augusta National, site of the Masters in Georgia). He referred to the suddenly-hallowed section of Arrowhead as the "Hallelujah Corner!"

In his post-game meeting with the media, Coach Marty Schottenheimer said, "We're finding a way to get it done, but I don't know if I can find a way to make it through 20 games at this pace."

This whole game was one to rejoice over, given its tilt-a-whirl momentum shifts, lead changes, and clock-teasing events.

Steve Bono hit Lake Dawson on a short touchdown pass for an early 7-0 lead, but the Raiders appeared fully in control after they piled up a 17-

7 lead on a pair of 1-yard scores by former Chiefs No. 1 pick Harvey Williams.

"Sometimes a team needs to know what to do when they are ahead," said Raiders Coach Mike White in an interview area outside the Oakland locker room. "I don't think there was conservatism, but I think maybe they were waiting for the clock to run down."

On the other side was a Chiefs coach who always admired the way the Chiefs played from start to finish. That was former Raiders Head Coach Art Shell, who wore the Red and Gold for the first time against the team for whom he labored during a Hall of Fame playing career.

With 13:32 left in the fourth quarter, Bono connected with Willie Davis to score from the 19. And then the Chiefs looked set to take command.

Dan Saleaumua picked off a pass deflected by Neil Smith at the Raiders' 22. But the drive stalled at the 6 with 2:38 to play, and Lin Elliott, who tied the score at 17-17 with 7:57 remaining, missed a field goal attempt from 24 yards, forcing overtime. A little over four minutes had elapsed in the extra period, and fans braced for the worst as the Raiders moved steadily toward field-goal range.

Fate intervened. Brown broke free, crashed into the umpire, and fell helplessly as Hasty snared the pass and sped to the victorious touchdown. This also became memorable for coach Marty Schottenheimer's impromptu display of elation: he was one of the first from the Chiefs' bench to make it to the end zone, and, kneeling, he bent and planted a big kiss on Hasty's forehead!

It was the second of three overtime wins for the Chiefs, half of their first six games, and part of the rush to a 10-1 start—avoiding the void predicted for them after Joe Montana announced his retirement in the spring.

James Hasty almost signed with the Raiders as a free agent before deciding upon the Chiefs. And he was glad he did! A year later, his 80-yard fumble return helped beat the Raiders.
(© Young Company)

Tamarick Vanover (#87) accumulated the most all-purpose yardage since Abner Haynes in the Dallas Texans' inaugural year, 1960. (© Young Company)

ONE MORE (OVER)TIME: OCT. 9, 1995
Attendance: 79,288
Temp: 68
Chiefs 29, Chargers 23... An "over" game... Vanover... Overtime... Overpaying.

This one lives large in Lamar Hunt's storage bin of memories because of a brief, tell-tale encounter with an exuberant fan after the Chiefs unbelievably had gone to overtime for the third game in a row at Arrowhead, and astoundingly had come away a winner for the third straight time!

This one featured a heart- and clock-stopping finish for Monday Night Football's worldwide telecast: Tamarick Vanover's thrill ride, 86 yards on a punt return that abruptly ended the proceedings. By strange coincidence, the play ended up in the left-hand corner of the end zone just as James Hasty's had three weeks earlier—the area that became known as "Hallelujah Corner."

Vanover, the wide receiver and kick returner from Florida State who had been drafted and then lured from the Canadian Football League, became just the second player in Chiefs history to return both a kickoff and a punt for a touchdown. Noland "Super Gnat" Smith did it during 1967-69 when the Chiefs played in Municipal Stadium, but Vanover accomplished his runbacks in the same season.

Pack Band director Tony DiPardo will remember this game for another reason. Of all the years he worked at Arrowhead, he missed this classic as the result of injuries suffered in an auto accident. But he wasn't forgotten by the team CEO and the head coach.

"Schottenheimer signed a game ball, and Peterson awarded it to me," said DiPardo. "It says 'You were with us in spirit' on the ball."

One fan among those who plugged into the Chargers action stopped Hunt on the sidewalk outside the south entrance where a crowd milled about after the game, seeking a peek at their stars and generally soaking in the surreal developments of the night and the season. This particular fan pulled out a $5 bill and thrust it toward Hunt, who said the man told him he wanted to pay extra "because ticket prices are not high enough for this kind of entertainment."

The entertainment didn't stop here. The victory, second in a string of seven in a row, had fans giddy over a 5-1 start that gradually rose to 13-3, the best record in the NFL. All of which made the final game so much tougher to swallow—the stinging 10-7 loss to the Indianapolis Colts in the first game of the playoffs at Arrowhead, a game bitterly memorable for all the wrong reasons.

P.S.—Lamar Hunt gave the fan his $5 back. It was the thought that counts.

RAIDER HATER IX:
SEPT. 8, 1996
Attendance: 79,281
Temp: 73
Chiefs 19, Raiders 3... All's right with the universe, Darth Vaders lag behind.

This was the 75th meeting between these two storied rivals and the all-time record going into the contest was remarkably dead even, 36-36-2. A six-game winning streak the Chiefs mustered against the Raiders lifted them to the break-even point. Except for the Chiefs, on two occasions in the 90s, no team in the NFL has been able to assemble a six-game winning streak against the Raiders.

The Raiders were without Jeff Hostetler, their

starting quarterback who was sidelined by a knee injury, so they turned to Billy Joe Hobert.

A 19-3 victory over the Raiders left Chiefs fans singing, "Ode to Billy Joe" on their way home. Hobert saw too much of Derrick Thomas who came up with two sacks, including one in the end zone for a safety.

James Hasty, who scored the winning touchdown the year before on an interception, came up with another big play by returning a fumble 80 yards for a touchdown.

The Raiders lost their last six games of '95 and started out the '96 season 0-2, leaving Coach Mike White in search of ways to overcome adversity. He said, "Those are the things that, when you haven't won for a little bit, weigh on your mind."

Enjoying one of the warmest receptions on the day was Chiefs placekicker Pete Stoyanovich, who made his debut at Arrowhead Stadium after the Chiefs obtained him from Miami. After a 47-yard attempt in the second quarter hit the right upright, Stoyanovich's first field goal in a Chiefs uniform occurred in the fourth quarter from 23 yards out.

From his first home game experience, Stoyanovich was left glowing. He said, "The atmosphere has been unbelievable. It's everything that everyone had talked it up to being as far as the college atmosphere."

Lake Dawson's promising season soon ended after this play against the Raiders in '96. A knee injury sidelined the third year player out of Notre Dame. (© Young Company)

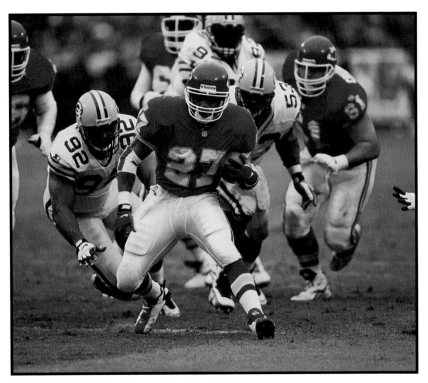

Although Marcus Allen averaged 4.8 yards per carry against Green Bay, the spotlight belonged to his eventual successor, Greg Hill (#27), who averaged 6.7 yards per carry. Hill scored two touchdowns against the Packers and rushed for 94 yards. (Photo by Tim Umphrey)

'DOG RUNS WITH THE PACK: NOV. 10, 1996
Attendance: 79,281
Temp: 30
Chiefs 27, Packers 20... Do me a Favre... Green Bay sent "Packing,"... A Cheese Meltdown

Later, Lamar Hunt would look back on this game as "the Super Bowl that wasn't, as far as we are concerned."

Although the cast on the field was different, the history of the first meeting between these two teams transcended upon the Arrowhead faithful who remembered Super Bowl I when the Chiefs were matched against one of the greatest dynasties of all time under legendary Coach Vince Lombardi.

The flicker of that flame which still existed from the AFL vs. the NFL days was exacerbated by the cover of "Sports Illustrated" in its NFL preview issue. Kansas City readers saw their beloved Chiefs on the cover with a prediction inside of a Super Bowl I rematch, a dream game for Chiefs fans who envisioned a revenge victory to ease the disappointment of what occurred 30 years earlier. And no matter what was to result in Janunary, 1997, Chiefs fans felt the specter of that Super Bowl aura in this regular season match-up.

For awhile, it appeared the pre-season prognosticators were on the right track after the Chiefs got off to a franchise landmark 4-0 start. The Packers came to town with but one defeat, making for a rare occasion when the Chiefs were underdogs at home according to the oddsmakers in Las Vegas. However, their determination is by numbers, not by what a player is made of, or what crowd noise at Arrowhead can mean to an opposing quarterback while trying to call the signals.

Cheeseheads abounded in the parking lots before the game (and inside a tent where a couple decided to get married amid Chiefs fever), and in scattered seating sections throughout the game.

Among them was Frank Emmert and his son who were from Superior, Wisconsin. The elder Emmert was not your typical cheesehead-wearing Green Bay fan. One year earlier, Emmert's life was spared when he protected his face with the wedge-shaped foam from the impact of a plane crash outside LaCrosse. Emmert was returning from watching his Packers play at Cleveland Stadium against the Browns. Literally, with a new lease on life, Emmert had continued to follow the Packers and his favorite team to different road sites and he came away from Arrowhead Stadium impressed.

"It was absolutely totally awesome."

As the pregame anticipation built to as high as it ever has, Emmert, wearing his arrow pierced cheesehead, mingled good-naturedly with the Chiefs fans. And he returned to Wisconsin as impressed with the Chiefs fans as he was with the home of the Chiefs.

"They (the Chiefs fans) knew we were going to get our butts beat. They had faith in their team. Of course, I was really razzing them and giving them a hard time, disbelieving that we would ever lose to K.C., but they treated us with the utmost respect both ways. Shoot, they gave me some salsa to bring home to my family."

The game lived up to the hype. The danger that league MVP Brett Favre represented at quarterback kept Chiefs fans unnerved into the final minutes, even though the Chiefs seemed in command of their eventual victory.

Regular-season firsts from the home opener, a 20-10 loss to the Miami Dolphins, Sept. 17, 1972 (after three home preseason exhibitions):

1st play: Jan Stenerud kicked off for the Chiefs against the Dolphins. It sailed into the end zone for a touchback.

1st play from scrimmage: Mercury Morris of the Dolphins, a delayed handoff around left end for an 11-yard gain.

1st tackle: Safety Mike Sensibaugh nailed Morris.

1st pass play: Bob Griese, incomplete, nearly intercepted by Chiefs linebacker Bobby Bell.

1st Chiefs play from scrimmage: Wendell Hayes ran off left tackle for a 1-yard gain.

1st pass completed: Len Dawson to Wendell Hayes, a swing pass that gained 18 yards to the 50.

1st touchdown: Dolphins wide receiver Marlin Briscoe, 14-yard pass from Bob Griese. The play was set up by Miami's recovery of a fumble by Ed Podolak.

1st rushing touchdown: Dolphin FB Larry Csonka, who also was the first back to gain 100 yards in a game at Arrowhead (118 on 21 carries).

1st Chiefs points: Stenerud, 40-yard field goal.

1st Chiefs touchdown in Arrowhead: Tight end Willie Frazier, 4-yard pass from Len Dawson. Frazier came from tiny Arkansas AM&N, and this was the only season he played for the Chiefs.

1st punt: Miami's Brian Seiple, 42 yards, return of 3 yards by Larry Marshall to the Dolphins 32.

Arrowhead 1sts from other games:

1st interception return for a TD: Jim Kearney vs. Denver, Dec. 3, 1972. Bobby Bell also ran one back in the same game, 61 yards. Broncos' quarterback Charlie Johnson threw both passes.

1st Chiefs late game-winner: Against Denver on Oct. 7, 1973, the Chiefs won 16-14 when Len Dawson passed first to Otis Taylor for 28 yards, and then to Ed Podolak for 21 and the score.

1st fumble runback for a TD: This one was sprinkled with lots of local flavor. Against Houston on Nov. 18, 1973, defensive end John Lohmeyer, who played at nearby Emporia State (Kan.), picked up a fumble by Oilers quarterback Lynn Dickey, a former Kansas State star, under pressure from tackle George Seals, who played at the University of Missouri. Lohmeyer ran it 19 yards to add to a 38-14 romp by the Chiefs.

1st kickoff return for a TD: There have been just three. None occurred the first 15 seasons. Paul Palmer (Temple) had the first two, both in 1987. The first came on the lucky 13th (Sept.) and covered 95 yards in a 20-13 win over the Chargers in the home opener. He ran one back 92 against the Seahawks in a 41-20 victory two days after Christmas. The longest belongs to Tamarick Vanover (Florida State), 89 yards.

Chapter 3
Coaches' Memories

Hank Stram

ALTHOUGH HIS TEAMS PLAYED BUT THREE seasons in Arrowhead, Coach Hank Stram's fingerprints appear all over the place. The glory-days Chiefs were showing the effects of age by the time they kicked off in their new home, dropping to eight victories, and then seven, and then five in their first losing season since the year they moved to Kansas City a decade before.

Still, Stram's ultra-success with the Chiefs during 1966-71 was vital to the campaign to have the stadium built, vital to the overwhelming ticket sales that provided the fever to fill the new stadium, and many of his personal touches adorn the team's football palace, too.

"It makes me feel good that our winning seasons and Super Bowls provided a springboard to building Arrowhead at a time when Kansas City was growing with a new airport, Crown Center, and all," Stram said. "I have a great sense of pride and satisfaction about that impetus, but mostly it's a great tribute to the fans. We sold 72,000 tickets before we pumped up the balls and screwed the helmets on in that great facility."

He was responsible for many of the design features of the downstairs affecting the players—dressing room, coaches' offices, meeting rooms, etc. "That was probably my stamp," Stram said. "It was a fascinating time, because even though we were going state of the art, many players had to deal with the sentimentality and melancholy of leaving dear old Municipal Stadium. They loved it there, on the grass with all those fans right on top of you."

The players' facilities had a European touch. Stram said the Chiefs were the first NFL team with a complete training room, including the introduction of the "big tub" that players became addicted to—an oversized whirlpool. Stram had been in London, England, scouting for soccer-style kickers when he attended a world championship rugby game. "I couldn't believe the way they hit each other with no pads, so I visited the lockerroom to find out how they dealt with all the bumps and bruises. The coach showed me their large

The Vince Lombardi trophy signifying a Super Bowl title, the prize under Hank Stram. (photo by Chris Dennis)

whirlpool tub and said that took the soreness out for the next week's game." So Stram went back to a friend in Florida, renowned strength coach Alvin Roy, and had him install one for the Chiefs.

Racquetball courts were also innovative. "I'd played since my days as a player at Purdue," Stram said. "It's great for reactions, reflexes, hand-eye coordination, and conditioning." Additionally, the Chiefs moved into a huge lockerroom with nothing in the middle "...so we could meet with the whole team and nobody could hide," Stram said. Other touches included a theater and great sound system.

Stram gets teased for being a ham over one of his early determinations—that the Chiefs would occupy the far (north) sideline, i.e., the sunny side of the field, so they would constantly be in the eye of the TV cameras shooting the game from the press box on the south side. "That way we were featured prominently for our friends and relatives all 14 games, instead of just half of them," Stram said. "I was amazed the way people around the country knew our players by sight, because they were always on camera. I also always thought it made things easier for the assistant coaches working in the press box to communicate and find the right people on the sideline facing them."

Ironically, part of the newness of Arrowhead raised concerns for Stram. "It was a glorious feeling, such a special place, but we didn't like the idea of practice in the stadium every day. (The Chiefs had a separate practice facility when playing games at Municipal.) On that synthetic turf, without a doubt we had the speed—Otis Taylor and the gang—and the kicking game with two of the best ever (Jan Stenerud placekicking, Jerrell Wilson punting). But I didn't want us to lose anything because of the elements."

Stram was hard-pressed to rediscover memories of specific games and moments at Arrowhead, aside with the one that everybody reveled in—the opener. "That first game, and the regular season opener against Miami, who had beaten us in the longest game to end the previous season, were very special, obviously," he said. "But primarily, my thoughts of the place are dominated by everything leading up to getting the stadium built. It will always linger in my life as happy memories, and it's always a treat to come back."

Hank Stram and his quarterback, Len Dawson. (© Young Company).

Paul Wiggin

Former Chiefs head coach Paul Wiggin (1975-77) found himself returning to Arrowhead Stadium often in a much different role than on the sideline, and he found a much different scene than during his tenure at the helm. (© Young Company).

As Director of Player Personnel for the Minnesota Vikings, Wiggin is perched in the press box often scouting the Chiefs and their opposition. What Wiggin has seen first hand, from inside and out, is the full transformation of the Chiefs into a successful modern franchise. It was a transformation that followed an uneasy road on and off the football field in the early days of Arrowhead Stadium.

"Unfortunately, when I was there, they were still coming off the pains of losing the old Municipal Stadium," said Wiggin from his office in Minnesota, where the Vikings have also undergone a stadium transformation. "I mean it was a beautifully done stadium, and there was every reason to love it, but there was something about that old tradition. There was a lot of tradition in the minds of the typical Kansas Citian and that was still surfacing."

Tradition that went hand in hand with winning. By the '74 season, when the Chiefs finished 5-9, Wiggin inherited a team that didn't match the magnificent facility the Chiefs called home.

In Wiggin's first year, 1975, one troublesome spot in particular was the right guard position. Because of injuries, the Chiefs tried 13 players at that spot.

The team records in '75 and '76 under Wiggin were identical to the record during Stram's last season, 5-9. By the midpoint of the '77 season when the team started at 1-6, Wiggin was replaced by Tom Bettis.

One of the classiest moments of the '77 season after Bettis, who was on Wiggin's staff, had taken over occurred outside Arrowhead Stadium. The Chiefs won their first and only game under Bettis, 20-10, over the Green Bay Packers. According to former Chiefs Public Relations Director Bob Sprenger, Bettis took the game ball to his former boss's house that day.

"The organization was run by really good people. We were at a time when the team wasn't very good and I guess I probably did enough things wrong, too, " said Wiggin.

"Lamar and Jack were always good to me even though they were the ones who had to pull the trigger. They were class people and I always respected and appreciated that."

What Wiggin witnesses these days in the parking lot before a game was unfathomable outside Arrowhead Stadium in the early days.

"In our situation here (in Minnesota), we don't have anywhere near what they have there because we don't have the parking facilities for the tailgating. Even though we've been a winner, generally, we don't have the energy and enthusiasm that they have there."

Paul Wiggin leads the Chiefs on to the field alongside (#14) Ed Podolak. (© Young Company).

(© Young Company).

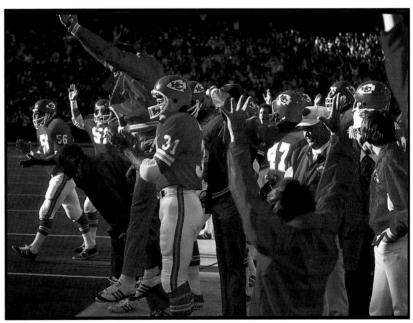

(© Young Company).

Marv Levy

Marv Levy interviewed by Bill Grigsby. (© Young Company).

Coach Marv Levy appeared to have the Chiefs turned toward a winning direction as the '80s set in, but labor strife and a player strike disrupted his reign, and his reconstructive effort blew up in his face. But he left several indelible impressions, including several "discovery" players—quarterback Bill Kenney, running back Joe Delaney, receiver Carlos Carson and several defensive standouts like Art Still, Gary Spani, Mike Bell, Ken Kremer, and Lloyd Burruss.

Probably the two most remarkable stamps Levy left on Arrowhead history were the use of the archaic "Wing-T" offense, and the replacement of a superstar, Jan Stenerud, with a nobody who became a superstar, Nick Lowery.

"That was one of the toughest decisions I ever had to make," Levy said of the selection of Lowery as placekicker to start the 1980 season, ending Stenerud's 13-year love affair with Kansas City fans. "It nearly got me lynched."

Lowery had been cut 11 times by eight different teams after his Ivy League college career at Dartmouth, and to Chiefs fans—and teammates,

for that matter—he was just another face, just another leg in a long string of wannabees who appeared in preseason camp, and then disappeared on the horizon as Stenerud proceeded toward the Hall of Fame.

"Every year the Chiefs had Jan and another kicker, just to save Jan's leg," Levy pointed out. "But when Lowery arrived, well, I had never, never had a kicker perform like he did in the preseason. He never missed, and at the end of practice he would kick field goals from 50 to 60 yards. Nick also was a bit brash and talkative, and I told him, 'Just cool it and kick.' I realized we had a unique talent, so I made the decision before the last preseason game. Jan was very disturbed. I don't blame him; I would have been, too."

(Author's Note: I wrote a column in The Kansas City Times following the ouster of Stenerud sticking up for him and challenging Levy's wisdom in making the move, especially so late in preseason when it would be difficult for Stenerud to land with another team. Marv Levy called me at home. He said he wanted to thank me for being supportive of Stenerud, that he deserved that. Levy was already one of my all-time favorites by then, as I had come to know him as an interesting, funny and totally classy man. Still, I was astounded that an NFL coach would take time to call and affirm an article that had basically just called him nuts.)

Levy went on to say of that bold move, "Although Nick had been magnificent in camp—he made kicks of 51 and 54 yards his first two attempts—the public didn't know much about him. Jack Steadman asked me, 'Are you sure?' When I cut Jan, the switchboard was flooded with calls. It was very gratifying five or six years ago at the NFL meetings when I was having breakfast with Chuck Knox, and Jan Stenerud came by the table and said to me, 'I'm not mad any more.' I've always admired him as a kicker and a person."

Use of the old-fashioned "Wing-T" offense also drew a lot of criticism Levy's way because it wasn't as exciting as a wide-open, passing game. That shocked many observers, since Levy had come from the pass-happy, longer-field Canadian Football League. The Chiefs moved like a slug with the ball, but, as owner Lamar Hunt exclaimed in looking back, "It worked!"

Worked is a relative term. Levy's five teams finished 31-42. But, the 1979 team improved by three games and played strong after a 1-3 start; the 1980 team went 8-4 after an 0-4 start, and the 1981 team started 6-2, beat the defending Super Bowl champion Steelers, and moved to the brink of the playoffs for the first time in a decade. "I believed the only chance we had to improve steadily was ball control and defense," he said.

Levy's first four draft choices in his first season, 1978, were defensive players, and the first three became starters—end Art Still, tackle Sylvester Hicks, and linebacker Gary Spani—and the No. 1 pick the next year was defensive end Mike Bell. While the defense matured, the rushing game

became No. 2 in the NFL in Levy's first season. Remarkably, five different backs gained 100-plus yards in a game that year—Mark Bailey 106 at Cincinnati, MacArthur Lane 144 at Buffalo, Arnold Morgado 115 at San Diego, Ted McKnight 104 against the Chargers at Arrowhead, and Tony Reed, who did it three times. At Arrowhead, Reed put together a 141-yard day on 16 carries against the Oilers, and added 114 at New York against the Giants and 121 at Seattle, and Reed became the Chiefs' first 1,000-yard back in 11 years.

Before he departed Levy had four more backs exceed 100 yards in a game—Mike Williams, James Hadnot, Billy Jackson, and Delaney five times in 1981 before his death the in 1983. "We always had people who could run the ball well," Levy said. "I loved the passing game, too, but it behooved us to work with what strengths we had."

In a retrospective look at Arrowhead memories, Levy said, "Truly, I think fondly of some of the lesser lights. Arnold Morgado scored a winning touchdown once for us. He became the mayor of Honolulu and asked me for a statement on video. I enjoyed putting together a 90-second clip of the game in which he scored that TD."

Among the many most memorable characters in Levy's brief tenure, Art Still holds a special place. "He was my first draft choice, and he was an unusual individual," Levy said of Still's reputation for marching to a different beat. "I'll never forget in his rookie year during a very hot preseason camp. He was pulling on these long, hot socks for practice. I asked him, 'Whose idea is this?'

"'Lamar Hunt,' he told me."

"'Damn good idea,' I said."

Running back Barry Word's nickname for Arrowhead Stadium, as seen through the eyes of opponents: "Terrorhead."

John Mackovic

(© Young Company)

"I can never forget my first game (Sept. 4, 1983) against the Seahawks. Chuck Knox was also in his first year (with Seattle). We won 17-13 in a typical knockdown, drag-out game with them. I came into Kansas City known as an offensive coach, and we used an unusual play that first game—Jewerl Thomas (who was around only that year) threw a halfback pass for a touchdown. But the rest of the game we played on their terms, got control of the ball and dictated the action."

"We won all our games against Seattle at Arrowhead. It demonstrates how there is such an advantage to continuity and knowing personnel in the AFC West, as opposed to games against the NFC opponents."

Mackovic told how, after severe frustration of a loss at home to the Raiders in 1986, he secretly prepared for the return game—for 10 weeks! "From that day forward (24-17 loss on Oct. 5) every day in practice we worked on three to five things the Raiders do. I didn't tell the players, but I had an asterisk on every practice script by those things—a play here, a defensive scheme there. I kept every script, and the week of the game out in

Los Angeles (Dec. 14) I held up all those practice schedules and told the team, 'What you don't know is, you've been getting ready for this game for the last 10 weeks.' We got them back."

The Chiefs won 20-17, followed it with another tough road victory at Pittsburgh, 24-19, for a three-game winning streak that catapulted them into the playoffs against the Jets on a 10-6 record and wild-card second-place finish in the AFC West. A month earlier the season had soured from a 7-3 start with a three-game losing streak, and Mackovic credits a resounding home victory over the Broncos, 37-10, and his ploy with the Raiders for salvaging the sagging spirits and setting up the climactic victory over the Steelers.

Mackovic was especially proud of one "discovery"—quarterback Bill Kenney. Mackovic was a quarterback himself at Wake Forest and he holds a reputation as a QB coach. Actually, Marv Levy uncovered Kenney as a for-real quarterback in 1981, starting him two seasons after he had carried the clipboard as No. 3 man for two years. But Levy still ran a conservative offense at the time, relying more heavily on the running game.

When Mackovic unleashed the heretofore unheralded, non-drafted quarterback full force in 1983 with the Chiefs' new wide-open spaces offense, Kenney stepped up with numbers that still topped the Chiefs' record lists for many years. "He had great vision and intelligence," Mackovic said. "That 1983 season was one of the best years an NFL quarterback ever had." It included Chiefs records (at the time) of most passes attempted, 603, and completed, 346, in one season; most attempted, 52 and most completed, 31, in one game; most consecutive completed (15, tying Len Dawson); most yardage in a season, 4,348, and most games with 300 or more yards in one season, seven, including four in a row. Kenney's career blossomed under Mackovic, but he battled Todd Blackledge for the starting position once Blackledge, the Chiefs' number one draft choice in '83, started getting his feet wet in the NFL. Kenney added several career passing records before retiring after the 1988 season when he lost his starting position under Frank Gansz.

Other Mackovic trademarks came from his off the field activity. He loved to read eclectic material (one of his favorites is Zen and the Martial Arts, by Joe Hyams), and he collected vintage and hard-to-find wines. But the legacy he left in his relatively short spin through Chiefdom was raising them out of the doldrums of 15 years and 3 days without a playoff appearance.

Frank Gansz

Frank Gansz, who was a big hit as special teams assistant coach with the Chiefs and then head coach for two seasons (1987-88), held typically high esteem for the arena that housed the team during his years in Kansas City. Gansz, who started the 1997 season back in the "Show-Me" State as special teams coach of the St. Louis Rams, said, "Great facility. Beautiful facility. I've always been impressed with it."

Little did Gansz know when he made his initial visit to Arrowhead Stadium in 1975 that some of his best football memories would be in store there for the man his players faithfully knew as "Crash." At that time, Gansz was in his last season as an assistant coach at Oklahoma State and Paul Wiggin was in his first season as the Chiefs head coach.

"We came up and my son (Frank Jr.) was with me. We were playing at the University of Kansas and we were up there to recruit the area and everybody was so nice to us," said Gansz, who took a trip to the office he later occupied as the head coach.

On looking back to that visit with Wiggin in his office, Gansz said, "When we went up to his office, I said, 'Man, I can't believe this office.' I was really impressed with it."

Gansz spent two separate tenures with the Chiefs, the first under Marv Levy in 1981-'82 as the Special Teams and Tight Ends coach. What later led to an NFL record 10 blocked kicks in the '86 season was precipitated by some of the big plays during Gansz's first tour of duty with the Chiefs. Although the emergence of Joe Delaney as an offensive threat electrified the fans at Arrowhead, the truth of the matter is that the backbone of what appeared to be shaping up as a solid team was the defense and the special teams.

Coming off a winning season in '81, there was hope. Then Air Coryell arrived for a game in the '82 season that stands out as one of Gansz's best memories. "They had (Dan) Fouts and one of the best teams in football. Gary Green blocked a punt for a touchdown. I'll never forget that game. That was very, very big in my mind." The Chiefs won, 19-12.

With Gansz around, the frontliners didn't mind contributing on the special teams. Albert Lewis was a prime example when the Chiefs capped their '86 playoff run with a win at Pittsburgh. However, it was a game at Arrowhead that planted the seed of what was to blossom against the Steelers.

Although the Chiefs' backs were against the wall in their home finale against Denver, 37-10 thrashing of the Broncos, in Gansz's opinion, the Oct. 26 game against Tampa Bay, when the Chiefs reached the halfway point of the season, was more pivotal.

The story leading into that game was not so much what the Bucs brought with them, besides the loud plaid sportscoat team owner Hugh Culverhouse wore in the press box, but what they were without since Bo Jackson elected not to sign with them and join the Kansas City Royals organization instead. While struggling with a 1-6 record, the Bucs also released two starters before the Chiefs game, tight end Jimmie Giles and wide receiver Kevin House. Their release meant the absence of two of the Bucs' top four targets for quarterbacks Steve DeBerg and Steve Young.

(© Young Company)

The Bucs' main problem to deal with that day was the Chiefs special teams, which turned out to be so important as the season progressed. Gansz recalled, "There were some times like against Tampa Bay where there were some big turn-around plays like when Albert Lewis tackled the punter. That turned the game around. It was a tie game at the time. It was the beginning of the second half. Those were some really big plays."

However, the magic from the special teams in '86 didn't successfully carry into the other phases of play for the next two seasons under Gansz as head coach and Carl Peterson was ushered in to turn around the franchise in 1989.

Marty Schottenheimer

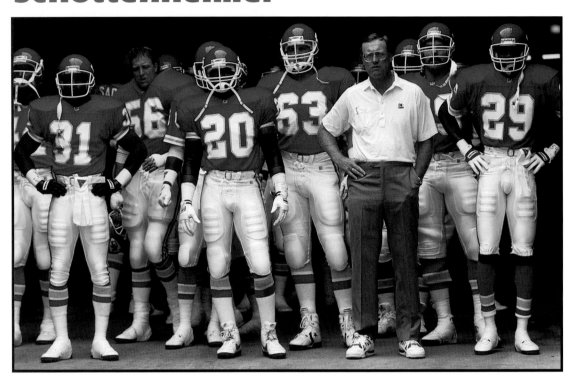

In his first eight seasons as coach of the Kansas City Chiefs, Marty Schottenheimer did not have a losing season. (© Young Company)

According to Marty Schottenheimer, the Dog Pound was awesome, but Arrowhead Stadium is the loudest non-dome in football.

With the old stadium in Cleveland razed, all that remains from the Dog Pound era are memories. However, as each week has unfolded under the coaching of Schottenheimer in Kansas City, another page is seemingly added to the list of memories.

Along with some of the games listed in the Top 25, Schottenheimer has added a few of his own favorite memories. One happened to be against one of his closest friends in the coaching profession, Don Shula. In the 1991 meeting against the Miami Dolphins, the Chiefs were still looking for their first win against them at Arrowhead Stadium. Since spoiling the regular season opener in '72, the Dolphins had returned only once. That was in '81 when Marv Levy was at the helm for the Chiefs and the Dolphins won, 17-7.

On Oct. 13, 1991, the Chiefs finally scored an Arrowhead win over the Dolphins, 42-7. Coming from someone who played linebacker in the NFL, the play that stands out in Schottenheimer's mind is a defensive one.

"Miami is about to score. (Dolphins running back) Sammy Smith dives over the top for a touchdown attempt. His elbow hit somebody and the ball fell to the ground in the end zone. Chris Martin, no. 57, our linebacker, picked it up and ran it 102 yards for a touchdown."

It brought the house down, much like the pre-game introductions each week, which still gives Schottenheimer a special feeling.

"I get a charge out of the pre-game introductions, especially when a guy like Marcus or Joe, the Hall of Fame name, is introduced. I get a rush," said Schottenheimer.

Then once the game is underway, the Chiefs head coach knows he has an extra element on his side, "The home crowd definitely affects a team, in perception as well as reality. What people don't really understand is that when you can't hear, you've got to fight frustration in addition to the confusion of the signals being called."

From Schottenheimer's staffs, other NFL clubs have come a calling. His top assistants have been lured away to establish themselves as NFL coaches. Pittsburgh Steelers Head Coach Bill Cowher, whose emotion got the Chiefs defense charged up during his three-year tenure as defensive coordinator, has been a frequent visitor both on the regular season schedule and in the playoffs. Before the '96 Monday Night Football game against the Steelers, Schottenheimer shouted, "Great rivalry in the greatest venue for football in America!"

All the signals since Schottenheimer arrived in Kansas City have pointed to a season provided with thrills.

Tony Dungy worked under Marty Schottenheimer for three seasons as the secondary coach before an elevated move to Minnesota as defensive coordinator. Eventually, Dungy landed a head coaching job with Tampa Bay.
(© Young Company)

(photo by Tim Umphrey)

At age 34, Bill Cowher was lured away from Kansas City to become the head coach of the Pittsburgh Steelers, but he was well-seasoned under Marty Schottenheimer. Cowher served as assistant coach for four years under Schottenheimer in Cleveland before joining him in Kansas City in 1989.
(© Young Company)

Dick Carlson

Dick Carlson called play-by-play of Chiefs games before and after the team called Arrowhead home. "You really can't appreciate Arrowhead Stadium without at least reminiscing about old Municipal Stadium," Carlson said. "The last year at old Municipal in 1971 provided some of the best memories that Chiefs fans will ever have. The Chiefs clearly were the dominant team in the old AFC coming out of the AFL days."

That changed with the last game at Municipal and first regular-season game at Arrowhead, both losses to the Miami Dolphins. "That was the changing of the guard," Carlson said. "...the beginning of the Dolphins' dynasty, and the beginning of the end of the Chiefs' dynasty."

Carlson saw the fortunes of the Chiefs unravel until his last season in 1977. During that downward spiral on the field, other cities borrowed ideas from the construction of Arrowhead Stadium. More spacious quarters for the home team was a popular feature, and one of the most memorable to Carlson because of all the interviews he conducted in the locker room.

"Up until that time not a lot of attention in stadiums was paid to the players' facilities, and locker rooms generally were pretty Spartan," he said. "When the Chiefs got over to Arrowhead they got these beautiful, wood lockers, carpet, and of course Chiefs red was everywhere. That locker room had to be four or five times larger than old Municipal Stadium.

"The kinds of things that jump at you, particularly with some perspective now, is how far ahead of its time the stadium was."

Wayne Larrivee

Former Chiefs radio announcer Wayne Larivee returned to Arrowhead on occasion in the radio booth of the Chicago Bears. During the 25th anniversary season he met with two problems—he left his media pass in Chicago, and he got caught in a massive traffic jam getting to the stadium. He sweated it out and arrived in time for the broadcast.

Although he missed most of the pregame buildup Larivee soaked in the most important part of the Arrowhead legacy—its staying power on the face of football stadium architecture. "Arrowhead is in amazingly good shape in terms of the physical appearance and the way it's been kept," Larivee said. "It's kept like Disney. Everything is clean. Everything is made to look new, and, boy, that's a true testament to the organization and the pride that Kansas Citians have in that facility at Truman Sports Complex. To this day, there's no place better."

Among Larivee's fondest memories was watching the Chiefs hold Hall of Famer Walter Payton to just 70 yards in 1981 (Nov. 8), although the Bears pulled out a 16-13 victory. Even fonder, a week later the Chiefs' budding star running back ran for 193 yards to help the team rebound to a 23-10 victory over the Oilers as 73,984 fans watched."

"He was amazing," Larivee said. "Marv Levy basically rode him to the first winning record (9-7) the Chiefs had had since the early '70s. He was a little guy, Joe Delaney, but, boy, what a tremendous heart he had." That turned out to be the only winning season Larivee would enjoy during his seven years at the microphone.

Kevin Harlan

As a broadcaster with Fox Network in 1995 Harlan's neutrality was apparent during a Redskins' 24-3 victory over the Chiefs, but the local fans never would forget his unbridled enthusiasm on their radios during 1985-'93. He left behind one of the most impressionable memories, the cry on big Chiefs gainers or defensive gems:

"Oh, Baby, what a play!"

It sprang from his excited call during the Monday Night Football victory over the Buffalo Bills on Oct. 7, 1991. Harlan was driving home with his wife, Annie, listening to Bob Gretz on KCFX postgame when a small cluster of fans called in and, on a count of three, screamed in emulation, "Oh, Baby, what a play!"

"It was just one of those things that came out," Harlan said of the trademark call. "I have a different call for everything, but for whatever reason, people kind of hooked onto that. And that night it was born. We developed it and the Chiefs used it in advertising, on the scoreboard, on T-shirts, and on hats. It was fun."

Harlan also introduced every kickoff at Arrowhed the same way: "Welcome to the most beautiful stadium in the NFL."

Measuring his thoughts for an Arrowhead retrospective, Harlan recalled the difference in travel time from home to the stadium in his first few years and his last few. "I remember how easy the drive was in 1985," he said. "I would leave my house in Prairie Village at 10 a.m. and get there in about 20 minutes. I just sailed right in. I'd do my show at 10:30 with the coach for a noon kickoff.

"After the new regime took over I had to leave the house earlier and earlier. To watch that change, almost overnight, was remarkable. That was the best part about being there… to watch going from literally the depths of the NFL to one of the best, if not the most successful overall franchise in the league."

Mitch Holthus

Mitch Holthus made his debut at the Chiefs mike in 1994 on what he said "…might have been the biggest game in Chiefs history at the time - the closest you can get to Super Bowl feelings in a regular-season game." That second game of the season featured quarterback Joe Montana against his former team that he led to four Super Bowls, the 49ers.

"I was feeling weak-kneed from the emotion, the tension, the awareness of how big the game was," Holthus said. "It was like the whole world was watching or listening to this one event. The whole scene was unlike anything I've ever seen. I got caught in traffic at 8:15 in the morning."

Kansas City savored that one from waking 'til long after sunset-a victory against the eventual Super Bowl winner. From that highest of highs, Holthus plunged to one of his deepest valleys two weeks later when the Chiefs, 3-0, fell to the underdog Rams 16-0, the only shutout in two years with Montana at QB. "It was almost like God was trying to show us both ends of the spectrum so we could respect it," Holthus said. "It was the lowest you could feel about a football game."

A season later the Chiefs provided many exciting finishes on the way to a 13-3 record. In one of those only Holthus will know what he said during the final seconds of a Monday Night Football victory over the Chargers, 29-23, in overtime. "We win on Tamarick Vanover's punt return, and my play-by-play call gets drowned out by a noise something like that of a 747 flying overhead. I remember not hearing anything but the crowd roar, and I thought it drowned me out. Turns out, (engineer) Danny Israel–who is terrific, and this is not to embarrass him–had six crowd microphones, and he was trying to mix them with my call. Inadvertently, in trying to neutralize the crowd, he turned me down.

"That was one of the most famous plays in Chiefs history that never got called."

Bill Grigsby

One of Kansas City's great ambassadors, radio personality Bill Grigsby - or "Grigs," as he is widely known - offers a unique perspective from being around the Chiefs since Day One in Kansas City. Take, for example, the closed restroom dilemma (page 38). Grigsby told his radio audience, "People seem to be leaving the game in groups. If they are leaving in alphabetical order, they must be down to 'P.'"

Grigsby had the inside scoop on certain player transactions, like the trading of popular, tough nose guard Curley Culp whose tenure in Kansas City ended abruptly in 1974. "Curley was a starter on defense," Grigsby recalled, "and he heard that George Seals, a non-starter, made more money than he did. So Curley got into a big row with Hank Stram over a raise. Culp got so mad he threw Stram's car keys down the elevator shaft. Henry traded Curley and a No. 1 draft pick for John Matuszak."

Another favorite Grigsby recall was the Jekyll-Hyde transformation of coach Marv Levy after one tough loss. A first-hand witness, Grigsby described what happened: "Marv was ashen after this loss. He went into his office, beat his head on the wall, walked out, adjusted his tie, and, calm and unruffled as he always was, he addressed the crowd, 'Hi, guys.'"

Grigsby didn't mask his feelings after the 1990 loss to the Seahawks on a touchdown pass thrown by Dave Krieg as time ran out. Play-by-play announcer Kevin Harlan asked Grigsby on the air, "How do you feel, Grigs?" To which Grigsby replied, "Too old to cry, and not quite sick enough to puke."

As an early arrival at Arrowhead Stadium on game days, Grigsby often encountered a lone figure seeking some quiet time - Joe Montana. Through all the high-profile commercials, marriage to TV personality Jennifer, and Super Bowl status, Grigsby saw a different person than the public clamored for - the antithesis of the other famous Joe Quarterback, known long ago as Broadway Joe.

"Joe Montana always came out to the stadium very early to have a little privacy and gather his thoughts," Grigsby said. "He'd get a slow tape job, and then walk the field in solitude. For as great a star as he was, he was a shy individual."

Not a tag ever applied to the effervescent symbol of optimism known to generations as "Grigs".

Chiefs Network radio team; (l to r) Mitch Holthus, Len Dawson, Bill Grigsby and Bob Gretz.

Chapter 4 Arrowhead: Not Just Chiefs Football

NON-CHIEFS EVENTS
THE AFC-NFC PRO BOWL...
YES, PRO BOWL GAME:
JAN. 20, 1974
Attendance: 66,918
Kickoff 1:13 p.m.,
41 degrees, 7 mph wind

THIS ENTRY IS SIGNIFICANT IN MANY WAYS. For one, it only happened once. For another, the AFC won, 15-13. Garo Yepremian of the Miami Dolphins—an all too familiar opposing name to Chiefs fans—kicked five field goals, nursing a sore left knee with an ice pack in between kicks.

For yet another, the attendance of 66,918 was the largest for the game in 20 years, and remains the third-largest in the 50-plus years of the matchup of NFL all-stars.

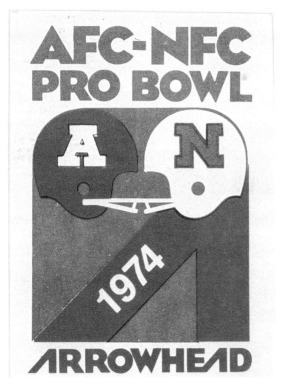

But what makes the presence of the Pro Bowl in Kansas City a wonderful story is how it came about. "We pretty much snowed the league officials," Lamar Hunt said. Pun intended, Lamar?

He enjoys recounting the tale of how he and Jack Steadman gathered extensive research with which to make their pitch for the game, which heretofore had been played in Los Angeles to increasingly sparse crowds. "We studied, a multi-year average picture of Kansas City weather for that date, January 20, and showed that the average temperature over that period was 41 degrees."

The league bit. Kansas City was awarded the game. On the Monday after the Super Bowl, as the all-star participants arrived, they stepped into one of the worst ice storms Kansas City ever recorded and a frigid temperature. What to do, what to do? Quickly, flights were arranged and the teams went to the sunny, warm climes of San Diego for their week of preparation.

George Toma and his groundskeeping crew went to great lengths to get the Arrowhead field readied. "At first," Hunt reported, "the ice was so thick we couldn't chisel it out of the seats or off the field." But, a warm front moved in on the day before the game as the players returned to the site.

Lo and behold, Sunday, Jan. 20, dawned sunny and blue, and by game time the temperature was—you guessed it—41 degrees. "Just like we told them," Hunt said. "Mother Nature delivered."

Game highlights:

The NFC took a 10-3 lead during the second quarter on the first of two field goals by Nick Mike-Mayer and a 14-yard scoring pass from Roman Gabriel to Lawrence McCutcheon. Yepremian pushed three more field goals through and the AFC led going to the wire. Mike-Mayer had watched a third-quarter attempt from 45 yards hit both the crossbar and an upright and fall away no good with the NFC leading 10-9 at the time.

With 1:41 left Mike-Mayer connected from 21 yards and the NFC led 13-12. But Yepremian was good again from long range with 21 seconds on the clock, sealing the victory. His kicks covered 16, 37, 27, 41 and 43 yards. Bob Griese passed the AFC into position for the game-winner with four completions in the final drive.

Turnovers pocked the game. Each side lost four fumbles, and the NFC intercepted Ken Stabler four times. Marv Hubbard, a Chiefs nemesis from the Oakland Raiders rivalry, gave the AFC offense oomph with 104 yards on 17 carries, and O.J. Simpson gained 76 on 19 runs. Floyd Little added 32 yards to the AFC's strong 220-yard rushing game in which there were no spectacular break-

aways (Hubbard's 18-yarder and Juice's 13 were the top gainers).

The most significant turnover was Elvin Bethea's hit on Gabriel, forcing a fumble that Phil Villipiano ran back 51 yards, taking the NFC out of a scoring opportunity. They had been at the AFC 1-yard line on second down before a penalty and then the fumble. Gabriel also fumbled earlier on 3rd-and-6 at the AFC 6.

Simpson thrilled the crowd with a 33-yard kickoff return, but he also fumbled the ball away twice. Greg Pruitt, had a 34-yard kickoff return and 24-yard punt return, and Hubbard lost the other fumbles.

The passing game was iffy, with Ken Stabler hitting just 2 of 15 for 19 yards. Griese in relief completed but 7 of 15 for 96 yards. Fred Biletnikoff, Jerome Barkum and Haven Moses caught two each. Ray Guy averaged 49 yards on his four punts for the AFC.

The NFC's vaunted runners, Lawrence McCutcheon (9 carries, 30 yards), Chuck Foreman (just 14 yards on 11 carries), and John Brockington (6 for 15 yards), went nowhere. Quarterback John Hadl from the nearby University of Kansas hit 4 of 10 passes for 33 yards, and Gabriel went 8 for 21, 138 yards. McCutcheon added 53 receiving yards to his day on four catches.

Dave Wilcox was a tackling demon for the NFC with 10 solos and an assist. Andy Russell led the AFC with 7 solos, an assist, a fumbled recovery, and a pass broken up. Future announcers got into the act: Bob Trumpy had the longest gaining pass reception for the AFC, 21 yards—which came on the winning drive with 49 seconds left—and he made two tackles. Nick Buoniconti made five tackles for the AFC.

Willie Lanier of the Chiefs had six tackles, matching Ted "The Stork" Hendricks. Center Jack Rudnay was the only other Chiefs player, and he saw some action as a substitute.

Yepremian said after the game, "I knew that Bob (Griese) could do it just as he did for us (Miami) all season, so I had to come through, too. There was a lot of pressure, but I couldn't let them down." He explained that he had strained his left knee when it buckled during warmups while both feet were planted. "It's very sore," he said, "but I am an athlete, and I can stand pain."

John Madden, the AFC coach, revealed his usual sense of humor, saying, "Now I am even (one win, one loss in the Pro Bowl), like Shula." Don Shula of the Dolphins was 1-1 in the Super Bowl at the time.

Losing coach Tom Landry of the Cowboys was baffled by the fumblitis. "I don't know why the ball would keep getting away from these great players. Perhaps the combination of moisture and cool air, after we had worked out in warmer weather."

What—41 degrees wasn't warm enough, Coach? Hey, the sun peeked through the overcast, the wind was still, and it was warm enough to keep a promise—and finagle the game into Arrowhead's lustrous setting.

Lake Dawson, watching a game from Lamar Hunt's suite while Dawson was injured and on crutches, recalled, "I remember my first game, against the Oilers (preseason, July 31, 1994), and everything in this place seemed larger than life. I didn't realize the scope. And it was so fast-paced, compared to the college experience. Here I was, on the field playing with Joe Montana and Marcus Allen—guys who were giants when I was growing up in football. I was in total awe."

The Lineups: 1974 Pro Bowl at Arrowhead

AFC

Offense
WR	Isaac Curtis,	Bengals
LT	Art Shell,	Raiders
LG	Gene Upshaw,	Raiders
C	Jim Langer,	Dolphins
RG	Larry Little,	Dolphins
RT	Winston Hill,	Jets
TE	Riley Odoms,	Broncos
WR	Fred Biletnikoff,	Raiders
QB	Ken Stabler,	Raiders
RB	O.J. Simpson,	Bills
RB	Marv Hubbard,	Raiders

Defense
LE	L.C. Greenwood,	Steelers
LT	Mean Joe Greene,	Steelers
RT	Paul Smith,	Broncos
RE	Elvin Bethea,	Oilers
LLB	Ted Hendricks,	Colts
MLB	Willie Lanier,	Chiefs
RLB	Andy Russell,	Steelers
LCB	Clarence Scott,	Browns
RCB	Willie Brown,	Raiders
LS	Dick Anderson,	Dolphins
RS	Jake Scott,	Dolphins

Kickers
PK	Garo Yepremian,	Dolphins
P	Ray Guy,	Raiders

Substitutes—QB Bob Griese, Dolphins; CB Robert James, Bills; RB Franco Harris, Steelers; S Jack Tatum, Raiders; RB/KR Greg Pruitt, Browns; WR Haven Moses, Broncos; G Larry Little, Dolphins; C Jack Rudnay, Chiefs; LB Phil Villapiano, Raiders; G Bruce Van Dyke, Steelers; DT Jerry Sherk, Browns; DE Dwight White, Steelers; WR Jerome Barkum, Jets; TE Bob Trumpy, Bengals; LB Nick Buoniconti, Dolphins; T Dave Foley, Bills.

NFC

Offense
WR	Charley Taylor,	Redskins
LT	Ron Yary,	Vikings
LG	Tom Mack,	Rams
C	Forrest Blue,	49ers
RG	John Niland,	Cowboys
RT	Rayfield Wright,	Cowboys
TE	Ted Kwalick,	49ers
WR	Harold Jackson,	Rams
QB	John Hadl,	Rams
RB	Chuck Foreman,	Vikings
RB	John Brockington,	Packers

Defense
LE	John Zook,	Falcons
LT	Merlin Olsen,	Rams
RT	Alan Page,	Vikings
RE	Claude Humphrey,	Falcons
LLB	Dave Wilcox,	49ers
MLB	Jeff Siemon,	Vikings
RLB	Chris Hanburger,	Redskins
LCB	Lem Barney,	Lions
RCB	Mel Renfro,	Cowboys
LS	Ken Houston,	Redskins
RS	Paul Krause,	Vikings

Kickers
PK	Nick Mike-Mayer,	Falcons
P	Tom Wittum,	49ers

Substitutes—QB Roman Gabriel, Eagles; KR Herb Mul-Key, Redskins; WR Harold Carmichael, Eagles; S Bill Bradley, Eagles; RB Lawrence McCutcheon, Rams; WR John Gilliam, Vikings; RB Jim Bertelsen, Rams; CB Ken Ellis, Packers; LB Jim Carter, Packers; C Ed Flanagan, Lions; LB Isiah Robertson, Rams; DT Wally Chambers, Bears; G Woody Peoples, 49ers; T George Kunz, Atlanta; DE Jack Youngblood, Rams; TE Charles Young, Eagles.

Officials—Referee Jack Reeder, umpire Walt Parker, line judge Don Orr, linesman Burl Toler, back judge Jack Steffen, field judge Charley Musser.

'VICTORY' OF ANOTHER SORT: MICHAEL JACKSON KICKOFF
July 6, 7, 8, 1984

The summer of 1984 broke new ground for Arrowhead Stadium, a spectacular three days of loud, vibrant, LOUD, swashbuckling–did we mention loud?–music and choreography and lights and gyrations that kicked off Michael Jackson's worldwide "Victory" tour. At the time it was the largest international concert tour ever pieced together.

In its concert configuration Arrowhead seated a smidgen more than 45,000 and it sold out three consecutive nights. And the noise might not have shown up on the Richter scale, but Jackson County neighbors for miles swear they could feel the vibrations as their sky was awash with the light reflections, a man-made *Aurora Borealis* (Northern Lights), of sorts.

The stadium's planners and developers and builders could be forgiven if they gloated, for this Michael Jackson spectacle bore them out on their

vision of multipurpose use of the facility. Clearly, from the outset, the stadium would be built for football only, as opposed to the cookie-cutter stadiums in Atlanta, Pittsburgh, Philadelphia, Cincinnati, among many, that were built to accommodate baseball, too.

Lamar Hunt's marketing department had long been charged with helping pay the freight with non-football events in the off-season (who can ever forget the monster truck and tractor pull events). The incredible Michael Jackson feat established Arrowhead as a viable site for other major concerts, such as The Rolling Stones, The Who, Elton John, Paul McCartney & Wings, Guns 'N Roses, Metallica, Ted Nugent, Pink Floyd, and U2.

People who worked to put together the huge event remembered Michael Jackson arriving at the stadium for rehearsals and performances and cavorting about town in an old beat-up van so that people wouldn't suspect who was in it. The stalwart Arrowhead maintenance crew had to tear out a wall so that the concert equipment could get through to the field, and they reconstructed it afterward.

Michael Jackson takes the stage at Arrowhead. (© Young Company)

Arrowhead crowd awaits Pink Floyd. (photo by Bischoff)

Bob Wachter, the director of stadium operations, said that the Jackson tour "went very smoothly." He recalled the first concert–"Elton John before he was famous, in the early '70s, and it was a get-your-feet-wet program for us." Two other concerts stood out in his recollections: the Rolling Stones, and Waylon and Willie.

"The Stones caused more operational challenges than any other event here, ever," Wachter said. "People showed up Tuesday and Wednesday for a Friday event. A sheriff in charge asked if we wanted to make them leave, but we said we'd try to service them and keep them happy. It was amazing–about 10,000 people in tents, RVs, station wagons. We told them they could stay, but they'd have to obey the rules. We gave them trash bags and told them to bring their garbage up to our office."

Wachter stayed three nights at the stadium with his staff. The last night, a staffer told him, "A whole bunch of them want to see you." Wachter said he thought, "Uh-oh." But he walked outside to find garbage bags stacked about 15 feet high. "It was amazing to us," he said.

Willie Nelson and Waylon Jennings performed in a heavy rainstorm. When lightning started flashing, Willie bailed. "But Waylon played on, right through the storm," Wachter said. He recalled a group of fans who worked their way about half a mile through the goo of storm sewers off Raytown Road to sneak into a concert, but when they surfaced in the southwest corner by climbing up six feet through a manhole, security guards caught them and escorted them out.

"We did a lot of homework," Wachter said of prepping staff and stadium for non-football events. "We traveled six months to various places looking for the right answers. There's a whole different set of rules for music than football. We had to change our thinking."

MLS GIVES ANOTHER KIND OF KICK TO THE 'HEAD
April 13, 1996

The most recent venture onto the horizon of Lamar Hunt's Arrowhead vision, is billed as "A Game for the Future." The Kansas City Wizards of Major League Soccer made their debut at Arrowhead on April 13, 1996. (Originally, they were called The Wiz; the name changed after the first season.) The turnout extended beyond the organization's wildest dreams. With but one gate open in anticipation of perhaps 12,000-13,000, the attendees actually experienced a logjam at overrun ticket windows, as 21,015 passed through the turnstiles for this inaugural event. "People complained, justifiably," public relations director Jim Moorhouse said, "and I was thrilled. It was a great problem to deal with."

The Wiz(ards) beat the Colorado Rapids in a sensational opening game, 3-0, giving rise to the "Digital Crawl," and then pushed on to a winning season and into the playoffs, finally falling to the Los Angeles Galaxy in the second round.

Wizards coach Ron Newman and his band of merry footballers (as they are known in all parts of the world except America) made the popularity of the new baby on the block a rousing success, featuring such crowd faves as Digital—can we ever forget his gleeful, playful crawling along the sidelines on his knees after a score?—and Preki.

The first game proved signature. The Wiz broke a scoreless deadlock with all three goals in the second half. It set a standard. The home team treated Arrowhead fans to an average of three goals a game that first season, the highest home scoring output in the league. And an average of 13,000 a game watched it, a remarkable figure for a market devoid of soccer ethnicity in its populace or World Cup experience in its history.

Digital scored the first goal, so appropo, since a ton of advance raves put the spotlight squarely on him from the get-go. Immediately he dashed to the sideline, plopped to the ground and began his crawl. Teammates followed behind in a train, and this centipede scene quickly made Digital a hit with his youthful exuberance and bright smile.

The Wiz caught widespread fancy with their one-name and nickname wonders—Digital from Zimbabwe, Preki from Yugoslavia—and others, like Californian Sean "Tower of Power" Bowers, who may have pulled off the MLS defensive play of the year. That play was one of several highlights during

On Oct. 10, the Los Angeles Galaxy started the Western Conference finals with a 2-1 shootout victory over the Kansas City Wizards, concluding the home season at Arrowhead Stadium. The Galaxy proceeded to eliminate Kansas City in the next game in Los Angeles. (© Young Company)

a first-round playoff victory over the Dallas Burn on a rainy, midweek night in September with 10,000-plus dripping fans in attendance.

With Dallas ahead 2-1 and just 15 minutes remaining, another Burn chip shot skittered toward the goal. Bowers sprinted 40 yards, slid dramatically, nicked his own goalkeeper, and knocked the ball off the line out of bounds at the last split-second before it found the net. The spectacular save set the table for the Wiz to score twice in the final 10 minutes, win 3-2, and go on to win the series in Dallas, advancing to MLS's Final Four. Kansas City lost the Western Conference finals to LA. But not before making an indelible imprint in the 25-year history of Arrowhead.

P.S.—Preki obtained United States citizenship and joined the U.S. World Cup team. The Wiz became the Wizards. And, they continued the 25th year celebration with their second MLS season, commencing in March of 1997.

Steve Miller (© Young Company)

PROMISE KEEPERS: APRIL 1996

A spiritual movement that started a couple of years earlier under the auspices of former football coach Bill McCartney, at the University of Colorado, booked Arrowhead for a weekend in the spring. The event, an enrichment and renewal gathering of mostly men listened to a long lineup of inspirational speakers, a concept borne out of McCartney's strong religious beliefs and sense of family values and the man's role in the home.

But nobody expected the incredible response that Kansas City drew to the Arrowhead. More than 140,000 attended the two nights. One attendee who took his son said the experience was "deeply moving...especially when all 70,000 people linked hands." The multi-purpose nature of Arrowhead took on new meaning with this exuberant gathering.

From the get-go, Arrowhead had to play host to events other than football to make it a viable economic enterprise. Eventually, activities ran the gamut from National Drum and Bugle Corps championships to large motor-sport competition.

Paul McCartney. (Photo by Tim Bischoff courtesy MPL Communications © 1993)

Motocross. (© Young Company)

Floor of Arrowhead awaits the Paul McCartney concert. (photo by Bischoff courtesy Paul McCartney)

Chapter 5 Hall of Famers and Their Memories

Lamar Hunt

WHILE IN HIS TEEN YEARS DURING HIGH school in Dallas, Lamar Hunt sowed the seeds that would lead him down an entrepreneurial path in professional sports, primarily football. Although educated at Southern Methodist in his hometown as a geologist, Hunt was captivated by sports and their allure to the public. And that path eventually led to the door of the Pro Football Hall of Fame in 1972. He was the first person to be inducted from the American Football League.

"…Architect, designer and builder of an impossible dream…," read part of the text of Bill Sulivan's introduction of Hunt at the Hall of Fame induction ceremony. The AFC champion team each year receives a trophy in his name.

"I was a sports fan in general," he said of his formative years. "But early on I loved fiddling with ways to attract fans to events, because I noticed that in America there were many chronic sports fans." Those creative juices spawned both the AFL, and, although he points out that it was inadvert, the naming of the Super Bowl.

"After the pro football merger in 1966 there was no think-tank session to come up with a name for the championship game," Hunt explained. "We didn't

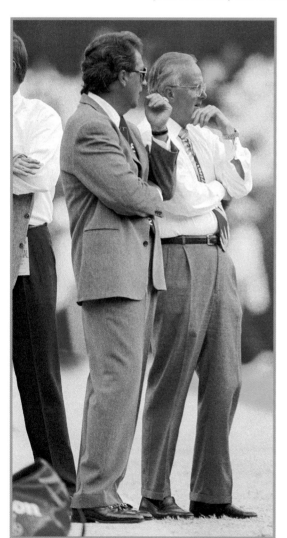

Carl Peterson and Lamar Hunt. (© Young Company)

have a big-time ad agency conduct market research to see if East-West Panorama Game or All-Time Football Game, or some such thing, would be appropriate.

"Rather the name came about accidentally during a meeting relative to the implement of the merger." The AFL had merged with the NFL, and in June the commissioner, Pete Rozelle, assigned a six-person committee to make recommendations on the logistics of the merger.

Hunt joined Billy Sullivan of the New England Patriots, Ralph Wilson of the Buffalo Bills, Dan Reeves of the Los Angeles Rams, Tex Schramm of the Dallas Cowboys, and Carroll Rosenbloom of the Baltimore Colts to hash out how the draft, preseason games, the playoffs and the championship game would be handled, among several issues. "During the course of those meetings, some confusion set in," Hunt said. "Should there be a one-week or two-week delay before the championship game, should it be on a home field or a neutral field, that sort of thing.

"The conversation went something like, 'Maybe we should let two weeks go by before the championship game.' Somebody said, 'Which game?' And I said, 'You know, the last game—the Super Bowl.' We all looked at each other, smiled, and within the committee after that we always referred to it as that."

Media picked up on it. Especially after announcers Paul Christman and Curt Gowdy referred to "Super Sunday" on the first telecast of the championship game in which the two major networks, NBC and CBS, took the same feed. "Rozelle thought it was undignified, and kind of corny," Hunt said.

So, the trophy, the game program, and the tickets for that first game bear the designation, "AFL-NFL World Championship." But, Super Bowl was the nomenclature out of everybody's mouth. Hunt said, "It was a kneejerk expression I came up with, based on something called a Super Ball that Norma gave our kids as a gift. It was a tightly compressed rubber ball and if you bounced it on concrete it would bounce over the house."

As a club owner Hunt remained always the supporter, the marketer, and the fan—hands-on in tending to all ideas and details to make his team and its home-game experience an enticing draw

Hunt with Jack Steadman
(© Young Company)

for the often fanatic support base. But never did he meddle with the product on the field.

Well, almost never. Asked if he had ever made a draft pick, Hunt responded, "No. But once I made a trade. In 1963 I traded our quarterback, Cotton Davidson, to the Raiders for their number one pick. Fortunately, with that pick we acquired Buck Buchanan."

Buchanan, a two-way tackle from Grambling, was the first pick in the draft, and he became a Chiefs legend on defense. In 1990, he was inducted into the Pro Football Hall of Fame.

Hunt, with prodding, will talk about his days as a reserve end in football at SMU. At Arrowhead Stadium he has appeared two ways as a football player.

One is in a makeshift kicking game in which he often would challenge his sons on the field several hours before Chiefs games. They called it "Kickball," and it started with Hank Stram, who loved to punt a football before games to let off steam. "I don't know where I learned it, or if we just made it up," Lamar Hunt said. His youngest son, Daniel, said, "It's a game of strategy, kids against the old guys, kicking the ball back and forth across the field between the sidelines."

The other football appearance is in a photograph sitting on an end table in the owner's suite showing him at age 7 playing with one of his brothers in a sandlot game. He is running the football against W. H. "Big Willie" Hunt. Lamar Hunt is identified in the 1939 photo by the nickname, "Chicken Hunt." To this day, Lamar Hunt remains as enthusiastic about the game of football as he was as a seven-year-old sandlot player.

Bobby Bell

Bobby Bell #78 jersey is among the eight Chiefs retired jerseys. (© Young Company)

Did anyone ever play outside linebacker better than Bobby Bell? Many astute observers of NFL football think not. And did anyone goad his original coach, Hank Stram, more? Many astute observers (teammates) think not.

"I loved pulling pranks on him," Bell confessed in looking back at his career that included three seasons at Arrowhead Stadium. "He loved to blow the whistle. So I got a whistle from trainer Wayne Rudy. We ran sprints in groups—defensive linemen, linebackers, defensive backs, and special teams. Hank would yell, 'Line up, let's go!' And we'd stop and go every time he blew the whistle.

"Well, before he could get it in his mouth, I blew my whistle and the players, who were dog tired, had their heads down so they didn't know it wasn't him, and they'd take off running. He sent word from Rudy to 'tell Bell to get in my office and don't be doing that to me.' When the same thing happened the next day, he yelled, 'That's it. Next toot on that whistle is a 50-dollar fine.' So I said, 'OK, Coach, you can have this thing.' It cracked me up. A lot of the guys were scared of him."

Bell played the game with such fury it was obvious no mortal scared him. He came from national honors at Minnesota, where he won the Outland Trophy as best interior lineman in the country. Because he was smallish for a lineman and because of the fear of the NFL signing him, he lasted until the seventh round of the AFL draft in 1963. But, small and all, Bell played defensive end his rookie season because the team was depleted at that position.

After moving to linebacker permanently for 12 years he intercepted 26 passes, recovered 15 fumbles, and became the first Chiefs player to enter the Hall of Fame in 1983. Although he grew up in North Carolina and played college ball in Minnesota, Bell found himself honored in the Missouri Hall of Fame in 1994. He maintains his home in Kansas City to this day.

"Most linebackers had a hard time covering the pass, but I was as fast as any flanker or split end, so I could cover any of them." As an example, Bell recalled the Raiders of the early '70s. "They threw a lot to their halfbacks, an Al Davis thing," he said. "One year they had Clem Daniels catching 7-8 passes a game. I watched him on film, and

Hank told me to follow him all over the field. He caught no passes at all that game. Once I ran with him to the sideline as he went to the bench, and John Madden said, 'What are you doing over here?' I told him, 'Hank said to follow Clem all over the field.'

"After that, the Raiders—and other teams—started to put a little flair in their pass patterns. It was a challenge to cover those halfbacks after that. As for wideouts, Lance Alworth and Paul Warfield gave me some problems because they were so quick and fast out of the gate."

In trying to recall any games that stood out above others in his years at the new stadium that closed out his career, Bell said, "Actually, even before Arrowhead, it's hard for me to single out games as special because I got up for every game. They were all special. Every game I played was a good game. I always played that way, plain and simple."

In fact, he said, he relayed that message to Lamar Hunt one year in a contract standoff (1969). "I said, 'I'm going to give you the ball off the defense three times on average a game. That's what I'll do for you, now go find two or three more who can do that.' I swore by that. I went almost a year without a contract, and Lamar mentioned that when I was inducted into the Hall of Fame."

So, in the memories of Arrowhead department, Bell's best shot was another prank on Hank Stram: "He loved to go up on this cherry picker, high on a truck, because he was short and he could look down and see practice better," Bell said. "Our equipment man, Bobby Yarborough, operated it and would lift him up there. One day I decided I was going to leave him up there. I disconnected the distributor cap.

"Practice ended, and Hank shouted down, 'Great practice. Everybody in. No running today.' We all broke for the tunnel. Inside, we all peeked out and Coach was still up there, with George Toma trying to get him down with a ladder. Next day there was a padlock on both sides of that cherry picker as big as my hands. 'That's your butt, Bell,' is all he said to me. I did a lot of crazy things to Coach Stram."

And he did a lot of crazy things to enemy offenses, making him an All-Timer in Chiefs history.

Bobby Bell (© Young Company)

Buck Buchanan

Buck Buchanan
(© Young Company)

Upon induction into the Pro Football Hall of Fame on Aug. 4, 1990, Buck Buchanan held no doubt about who would present him at the ceremony: his former coach with the Chiefs, Hank Stram. Buchanan arrived at that decision almost from the moment he learned of the honor.

Buchanan had other considerations. He might have gone with his coach from college days at Grambling, Eddie Robinson, the winningest college coach of all time who molded Buchanan as a prototype lineman. Buchanan played offense and defense under Robinson, and at 6-7, 287 pounds Buck starred as a defensive tackle through 13 seasons with the Chiefs.

Buchanan also considered Lamar Hunt, the club owner who traded the Chiefs' quarterback in 1963, Cotton Davidson, for the No. 1 draft pick with which they selected Buchanan. During an interview one week before the induction ceremony at Canton, Ohio, Buchanan disclosed his thoughts about selecting Stram as his presenter. "I had decided quite some time ago that Hank would be the person to introduce me," Buchanan said.

"I did think about Coach Robinson a lot and I really contemplated Lamar, too, and it was a very tough choice. But I just thought in my heart that because Hank coached me most of my career in professional football he should be the one. I talked to my mother about it, and some friends. She is a great fan of Hank, so that had something to do with influencing me a little bit.

By the time Buchanan accepted his Hall of Fame ring later that year at Arrowhead Stadium, he had undergone treatment in his battle against cancer. Georgia Buchanan, his widow who continued to run All-Pro Construction-the business that Buck founded-experienced one of the most moving moments of her life at that presentation, basking in the love that fans and former teammates showered on him one more time on the Arrowhead field.

"The most special Arrowhead moment to me," Mrs. Buchanan said, "was when they gave Buck his Hall of Fame ring. All of the former players who were there carried him off the field." That included men who introduced them when she was a school teacher living in the same apartment complex as Otis Taylor, Bobby Bell, and Sandy Stephens.

That was Buchanan's last appearance at Arrowhead, because when the club decided to retire his jersey No. 86 a year later, he was too ill to attend that ceremony. Cancer took his life shortly thereafter on July 16, 1992, at age 51. "They retired his jersey and presented it to me standing alongside Jan Stenerud and Willie Lanier," Georgia Buchanan said. "He was very pleased because he was told about it just before his death."

When Buck died, Mrs. Buchanan learned even more about how special the Hunts were in his life. "Let me tell you how special Norma and Lamar Hunt are," she said. "At Buck's death, Lamar was en route to Dallas. As soon as she heard the news she told him, and he came back to Kansas City immediately. Lamar stayed three days in my home answering the telephone and the door. And he called in his administrators to make sure Buck's funeral plans were followed."

Before he became ill, Buchanan was the driving force behind a fundraiser that became known as the Buck Buchanan Special Olympics Celebrity Sports Carnival. As the celebrity chairman his name remained stamped on the event in perpetuity after his death, just has it has remained in Chiefs annals.

Len Dawson

Len Dawson became an institution in Kansas City, and eventually a Pro Football Hall of Fame inductee, primarily for the part of his career that preceded the opening of Arrowhead. Those exploits in quarterbacking the finest array of Chiefs ever assembled (five Canton Hall of Fame players, plus seven Chiefs Hall of Famers) during 1962-75 actually helped fortify the movement to build a new stadium, and provide excitement that helped turn out the voters for the bond issue.

None of the individual or collective legacies of championship Chiefs ever faded (and, in fact, have grown all the more legendary with time, given the dip in fortunes throughout most of the '70s and '80s that left fans clinging to and longing for a return to the old days and ways). As bright as the eternal "Fame" lights glow, none has sustained the brilliance of Dawson's, because he moved from the field to the booth—as color commentator on Chiefs radio, local TV and as host of the longest continuously-running program on cable TV ("Inside the NFL" on HBO).

He left behind a long trail of franchise career records (passer rating, attempts, completions, completion percentage, passing yards, and touchdowns) and American Football League passing titles (four). To think that after a sterling career at Purdue where he was a protégé of his future pro coach, Hank Stram, and where he led the Big 10 in passing and total yardage three years, Dawson languished several years on the bench of the Pittsburgh Steelers, who drafted him No. 1 in 1956, and the Cleveland Browns.

Once he skipped to the upstart "other" league, Dawson helped mold the Chiefs into a year-in, year-out challenger to the throne. They ascended to the AFL championship in 1962, 1966, and 1969, and Dawson became MVP of Super Bowl IV for leading the 23-7 upset victory over the Minnesota Vikings on Jan. 11, 1970.

Although Dawson played but four seasons in the new environs, he holds lasting memories of the transition era. "The main impression that sticks with you through the years," he said, "is simply the incredible difference between our new facilities and the old ones at Municipal Stadium. It was so plush at Arrowhead that some of the guys would rather have stayed at the stadium than go home. Wilbur Young loved to play racquetball, and then relax in the sauna and steam rooms.

Hank Stram and Len Dawson confer to discuss the next play. (© Young Company)

Bill Grigsby and Len Dawson share football stories at the 101 banquet, an awards dinner that honors top Chiefs performers and the best of the NFL each season. (© Young Company)

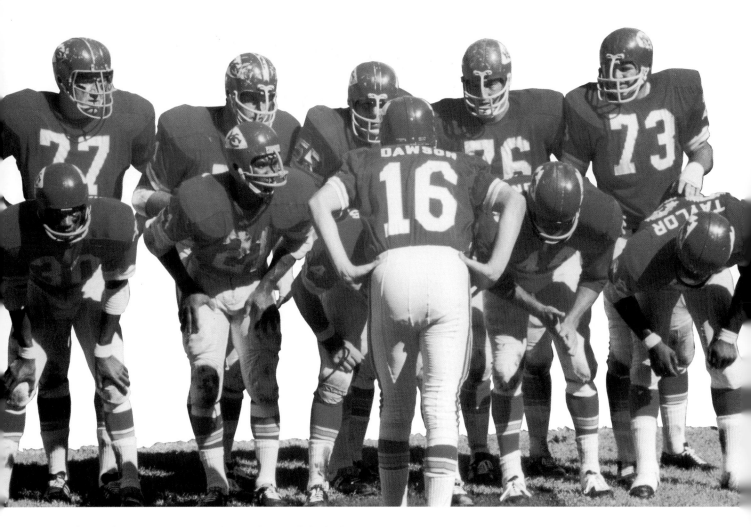

Nobody loitered around the locker room."

Dawson recounted how in old Municipal the players had to walk up steps to concrete ramps that led up to the dressing quarters. Arrowhead featured ramps leading directly from the meeting rooms and dressing room to the field.

He said he can also all but feel the pain of artificial turf after all the years, too. "We had no practice facility at Arrowhead," he said. "That synthetic turf pounded on you hard. It was tough playing there."

As with everybody who was present on opening day in 1972, Dawson speaks in awe of the splendor. "We had played for years in front of about 50,000 maximum, and to go in there with half-again as many people in that packed house for the first time, it was awesome," he said. "Even our

opponents were in awe."

Dawson also recalled Stram's dismay over players distracted in practice one day. "There was to be a rock concert, and the band was practicing. We were supposed to be hearing fight songs and polkas over the public address, but more guys were paying attention to the rock music, and Stram was beside himself."

Dawson kept fans' hopes aroused when, instead of a rumored retirement, he signed a two-year contract. But injuries beset him soon thereafter, and defeat beset the Chiefs. Dawson remains at the pinnacle of Chiefs' quarterback history.

Willie Lanier

The night before attending a Chiefs game in 1996, former Chiefs great Willie Lanier had been at defensive back Brian Washington's house watching heavyweight boxing champion Evander Holyfield fight. Lanier revealed something of his own personal credo as he talked about the champ: "It's good to watch Holyfield focus and do his work. He's not intimidated. Why? Because he's a man of God."

The prototype of a slam-tackling, wide-roaming middle linebacker—the best MLB in the first 75 years of the NFL—Willie Lanier was, by his own account, completely focused, and never intimidated. "In football, like any game, like any walk of life, if you stay focused, execute, do your job—you win. It doesn't matter what anyone else says."

In 1994 a pool of long-time observers of the NFL says that Lanier, along with teammate Jan Stenerud, was deserving of a position on the 75th Anniversary All-Time Team. Lanier came to the Chiefs in the second round of the 1967 draft out of Morgan State in his home state of Virginia; he played 11 seasons, displaying a fierce tackling style that was the bane of running games, ranging for 26 intercepted passes, and recovering 15 fumbles. All of that earned him induction into the Hall of Fame in 1986.

His responses to queries about his memories of six seasons played at Arrowhead Stadium offered insight into the intensity with which he etched a permanent mark on Chief history. For example, when asked about any highlights that might have occurred during the week of practice between games (several former Chiefs from the old days mentioned methods and antics of coach Hank Stram), Lanier said, "None would stand out above another, because I played in practice every day the same way I played in games. I came to work, and I worked hard."

And reflecting on highlight games was as tough for him (the Chiefs were 15-26-1 at Arrowhead during Lanier's days there) as the other Hall of Famers who spent much of their careers attaining recognition of the highest order before Arrowhead was built. Built, indeed, in part because of their earlier contributions. The last time the eventual Hall of Fame players all were together at Arrowhead was 1974—just the third year in the stadium. Bobby Bell retired after that

The game face of hard-hitting Hall of Famer Willie Lanier.
(© Young Company)

season, and Len Dawson and Buck Buchanan followed one year later.

One play stuck with Lanier through the years, possibly because it occurred against the reviled Raiders. During a 42-10 wipeout at home in 1975 Lanier set up a touchdown. "I was on the slot side and I intercepted a pass and ran 70 yards from our 20 to about their 10. I remember because it

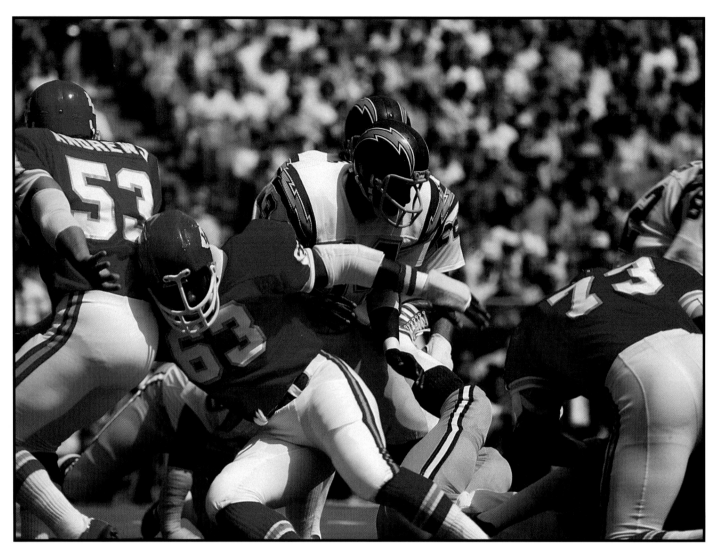

Willie Lanier at work against the San Diego Chargers. (© Young Company)

was a day that we had a few big plays that shifted the entire game."

Otherwise, he, like most, was forthcoming with vivid recollections of the first game that counted in the packed new house. "We were the first win for the Dolphins in 1972 (20-10) going toward their undefeated season. The game wasn't about football. It was about the 95-degree temperature. We were seated on the other side (north sideline, a result of Hank Stram's desire to have his team facing into the TV cameras), so we were going to have the worst of it.

"Bob Stein, a backup linebacker, found a thermometer and put it on the turf, and it read 125 degrees. During the second quarter Bob Griese started scrambling a lot. I looked into the eyes of our defensive linemen, and they were not home. They were drained. All the while, the Dolphins were in the shade on the other side of the field—they had it 10 degrees lower than we did. You could just tell when our energy level was sapped."

Lanier's success on the field translated to his life in business after he left the field. He built a new career dealing in capital market activities back where it all began for him in Richmond, Va.

Jan Stenerud

He revolutionized placekicking in the NFL, pure and simple. Well, not so pure. Stenerud, known more as a prolific ski jumper at Montana State University who had played soccer in his native Norway, refined the sidewinder, soccer-style kick-off, point-after, and field goal like no other. Some would say he defined it.

Stenerud was firmly entrenched five years into his history-making career, when the Chiefs entered Arrowhead Stadium, and he worked there during its first eight seasons on the way to the NFL record for career field goals, second place all-time in points scored, and a spot in the Pro Football Hall of Fame. Inducted in 1991, Jan was the first-ever to enter the Hall as a pure place-kicker; others like George Blanda, the only player to score more points (he had many as a quarter-back), and Lou Groza played other positions, too.

Steneruds most famous kicks occurred before Arrowhead came about, including a 48-yard field goal in the Super Bowl IV victory over the Vikings, and he was involved in one of Arrowhead's darkest moments when he, as one of the ring of extremely popular Chiefs borne of championship achievements, got released unceremoniously late in the preseason of 1980. Coach Marv Levy boldly sent Stenerud to seek employment elsewhere (which he found in Green Bay for four years and Minnesota for two before retirement), replacing a legend with a guy who had been cut repeatedly by other teams, Nick Lowery. "Marv caught more hell over that," Stenerud said, "because I played six more years."

That aside, Stenerud still enjoyed some terrific moments at Arrowhead that he relished in the rehashing. Certainly the first one, the preseason meeting with St. Louis. "After the disappointment of Christmas (1971 playoff loss to the Dolphins in the infamous "Longest Game"), the crowd gave us a standing ovation as if to say, 'We're still for you.' With all the hoopla, the town was on fire."

He recalled a 1973 victory at home over the Raiders in which Bubba Smith blocked three of his field goal attempts. "But I also kicked three, and Willie Lanier scored a touchdown and we beat them (16-3)," Stenerud said.

Other Stenerud highlights at Arrowhead:

- Monday Night Football, Nov. 12, 1973, against the Chicago Bears, a 19-7 victory. "…Great,

great night," Stenerud said. "Norwegian national television showed up for the first time. The Bears had Abe Gibron coaching, Bobby Douglass at quarterback, a local favorite (from El Dorado, Kans., and the Kansas Jayhawks). I kicked four field goals in the first half and it was 12-0. Before the last one the clock ran out as we tried to place the ball, but a Bears defensive lineman inadvertently stopped the clock. Gibron went crazy and ran onto the field. We won, and Norwegian fans then thought every game was like that."

- He lamented the departure of Hank Stram as head coach after the 1974 season. "When you

Jan Stenerud still holds the Chiefs record for the most field goals attempted at 436.
(© Young Company)

:53 WELCOME CHIEFS ALUMNI

Stenerud receives his Hall of Fame ring from Executive Director Pete Elliot. This was one of the last times that all six Chiefs Pro Football Hall of Famers were photographed together. (© Young Company)

allude to the getting the stadium built, the names that most often come up are Roe Bartle and Dutton Brookfield and Charles Deaton and Jack Steadman. And there were many involved in those great times. But one person with no shadow of a doubt had incredible influence on the coming of Arrowhead—Hank Stram. He ran everything; he was the supreme authority with our team. I'm saying this as strong as I can: if there hadn't been a Hank Stram, there wouldn't be an Arrowhead Stadium. He was as strong in Kansas City as Vince Lombardi was in Green Bay."

• His own departure. "I remember it clearly. Every year they would bring in another kicker to keep me challenged. But this time Levy didn't like the way I kicked. He kept saying, 'Not

high enough, not fast enough.' Well, they don't give points for fast and high. But Marv had been a special teams coach for George Allen, and he knew enough to be dangerous. I understand that he wanted his own people, and a younger team. He was a very smart man, and, oh, could he yell at officials. He ranted and raved."

Following retirement, Stenerud worked in client relations for an architectural firm and during the silver anniversary year of Arrowhead he moved to Colorado Springs, ending three decades of residence in the Kansas City area. But he really never left, not then, not in 1980, in the minds and hearts of Chiefs fans who have lionized that Super Bowling Stram band. Even when other teams had him, Kansas City got a kick out of Jan.

CHIEFS HALL OF FAMERS IN ARROWHEAD ERA

Bobby Bell, Linebacker, 1963-74
Ed Budde, Guard, 1963-76
Buck Buchanan, Defensive tackle, 1963-75
Deron Cherry, Safety, 1981-91
Len Dawson, Quarterback, 1962-75
Dave Hill, Tackle, 1963-74
Lamar Hunt, Founder
Willie Lanier, Linebacker, 1967-77
Jim Lynch, Linebacker, 1967-77
Ed Podolak, Running back, 1969-77
Jack Rudnay, Center, 1970-82
Hank Stram, Head coach, 1960-74
Jan Stenerud, Placekicker, 1967-79
Otis Taylor, Wide receiver, 1965-75
Emmitt Thomas, Cornerback, 1966-78
Jim Tyrer, Tackle, 1961-73
Jerrel Wilson, Punter, 1963-77

Those who did not perform at Arrowhead:
10—Mack Lee Hill, Jerry Mays,
Fred Arbanas, Johnny Robinson,
Chris Burford, E.J. Holub, Mike Garrett,
Abner Haynes, Sherrill Headrick,
Curtis McClinton.

CHIEFS MOST VALUABLE PLAYER

1979 Gary Barbaro, Safety, Nicholls State
1980 Art Still, Defensive End, Kentucky
1981 Joe Delaney, Running Back, Northwest Louisiana State
1982 Gary Green, Cornerback, Baylor
1983 Bill Kenney, Quarterback, Northern Colorado
1984 Art Still, Defensive End, Kentucky
1985 Lloyd Burruss, Safety, Maryland
1986 Albert Lewis, Cornerback, Grambling
1987 Carlos Carson, Wide Receiver, Louisiana State University
1988 Deron Cherry, Safety, Rutgers
1989 Christian Okoye, Running Back, Azusa Pacific
1990 Steve DeBerg, Quarterback, San Jose State
1991 Derrick Thomas, Linebacker, Alabama
1992 Neil Smith, Defensive End, Nebraska
1993 Marcus Allen, Running Back, Southern Cal
1994 Derrick Thomas
1995 Marcus Allen
1996 Mark Collins, Cornerback/Safety, Cal State-Fullerton

MACK LEE HILL ROOKIE AWARD

1966 Mike Garrett, Running Back, UCLA
1967 Jan Stenerud, Placekicker, Montana State
1968 Robert Holmes, Running Back, Southern U.
1969 Jim Marsalis, Cornerback, Tennessee State
1970 Jack Rudnay, Center, Northwestern
1971 Elmo Wright, Wide Receiver, Houston
1972 Larry Marshall, DB/Kick Returner, Maryland
1973 Gary Butler, Tight End, Rice
1974 Woody Green, Running Back, Arizona State
1975 Walter White, Tight End, Maryland
1976 Gary Barbaro, Safety, Nicholls State
1977 Gary Green, Cornerback, Baylor
1978 Don Parrish, Nose Tackle, Pittsburgh
1979 Bob Grupp, Punter, Duke
1980 Eric Harris, Cornerback, Memphis State
1981 Lloyd Burruss, Safety, Maryland
1982 Les Studdard, Center, Texas
1983 David Lutz, Tackle, Georgia Tech
1984 Kevin Ross, Cornerback, Temple
1985 Jeff Smith, Running Back, Nebraska
1986 Dino Hackett, Linebacker, Appalachian State
1987 Christian Okoye, Running Back, Azusa Pacific
1988 James Saxon, Running Back, San Jose State
1989 Derrick Thomas, Linebacker, Alabama
1990 Percy Snow, Linebacker, Michigan State
1991 Tracy Simien, Linebacker, Texas Christian
1992 Willie Davis, Wide Receiver, Central Arkansas
1993 Will Shields, Guard, Nebraska
1994 Lake Dawson, Wide Receiver, Notre Dame
1995 Tamarick Vanover, Wide Receiver/Kick Returner, Florida State
1996 Reggie Tongue, Safety, Oregon State

Chapter 6
The Carl and Marty Era

HE 13TH IN THIS SUBPLOT IS A GOOD-LUCK day in Chiefs history in 1988 (it wasn't a Friday). A November chill bit into the smattering of ne'er-die fans scattered around the Arrowhouse. Sitting among them, anonymously, unnoticed, was a man who now can't walk anywhere in the city without being recognized. Nobody knew who he was that day, other than just one more person with enough football running through his veins to want to see a pro game on a cold Sunday.

More accurately, he was wandering among them, observing the entire scene–pregame outside the stadium, pregame and halftime ceremonies, message board, band, cheerleaders, the works, in detail. Had the fans known they would have been wondering if Carl Peterson saw Arrowhead Stadium that day as half full, or half empty? (The Chiefs won that day on a last second field goal by Nick Lowery.)

Certainly it took no great perceptive power to recognize that a pall hung over the arena, the result of yet one more revival gone sour, one more coaching regime filled with promise gone dead. Marv Levy had played Moses to this red sea of fans, but, after a glimmer of radiance a player strike did him in. John Mackovic provided the next guiding light, and teased with a playoff berth, but was fired.

Frank Gansz seemingly had the answers. He was a bundle of energy in charge of special teams, and they created a lot of positive commotion and generated a lot of attention around the NFL. His first year, 1987, the Chiefs won four exhibition games, and carried the momentum into a season-opening victory over San Diego. But while some players swore *by* him, after swearing *at* Mackovic, Gansz's level of enthusiasm ultimately did not parlay into a level of excellence on the field when he was the head man.

So, what greeted the anonymous visitor, Carl Peterson, planted in the stands by Jack Steadman and Lamar Hunt to assay and assess, was a melange of doleful fans weary of their woebegotten team that had piled up 19 losses and a tie in 25 games. "A losing attitude permeated this place," Peterson recalled.

That aside, he took the optimist's view: half full. "I quietly observed that in spite of its age Arrowhead was still, and remains, state of the art. I got excited thinking about the potential for refilling this venue, for looking out and seeing 79,400 people in a sea of red. Even though it was the third-largest stadium in the NFL located in the fourth-smallest market, that challenge, that potential, invigorated me."

He made a pact with the Chiefs and brought that vigor to Kansas City immediately on Dec. 19, one day after the 1988 season ended, becoming President, General Manager and Chief Operating Officer. Shortly thereafter, Peterson received a telephone call from a coach who also sensed from afar, as an opponent, the possibilities in Kansas City. Marty Schottenheimer became available because of a fallout with the owner in Cleveland—"I owe a debt of gratitude to Art Modell," Peterson said—and Peterson, who had coached as an assistant against Schottenheimer, snapped him up.

Together, they created a regime like no other in Chiefs history, and restored the belief that the Super Bowl is not outside of the Chiefs' reach.

Peterson's charge was twofold: One, draw on his football coaching background to put together a

Marty Schottenheimer talks football with Carl Peterson who was also a coach before becoming an executive. (© Young Company)

staff that would identify, select and sign the best talent available from every source, from draft to trade to all those different kinds of free agents.

Two, draw on his experiences in the marketing and business of football to refill the stadium, and hire creative staff to fulfill that mission, too. Which begs the age-old chicken-and-egg question.

You might think that a winner must come first, but the Peterson-Schottenheimer combination showed that, even without an immediate smash hit, fans will turn out, albeit tentatively, on promise. Peterson's flair in the front office promised excitement and anticipation, both in the talent he procured (the first draft produced linebacker Derrick Thomas, who registered his trademark immediately—10 sacks and Pro Bowl selection, which became a perennial) and in the pizzazz at the ball park. Lots of heads rolled along the way—remember War Paint, the horse?—so his flair wasn't always popular at first, but nobody could argue, given the often-dreary past.

And on the field Schottenheimer's past promised the playoffs. Nobody doubted that his team would be there, and soon. It took two seasons, and then went uninterrupted six straight years until an abrupt (and very unexpected) dent in the Super Bowl plan in 1996. Never at Arrowhead had the expectation risen so high as in 1995, when, coming off the best regular season record in the NFL, 13-3, the Chiefs fell with a miserable thud at home against the upstart Indianapolis Colts.

Still, the Carl and Marty era had produced what it promised—a contender, year in and year out, building toward the ultimate prize. That building phase progressed rapidly with eight victories the first year, doubling the previous year's successes, and then steadily, stealthily, into an 11-game winner the next, laying the foundation to becoming a playoff regular during the next three seasons. At that time the braintrust sent tremors throughout the NFL community with two spectacular moves that underscored the bravado and commitment with which Kansas City changed the way it looked on the pro football map: In 1993 the Chiefs brought Joe Montana and Marcus Allen to town.

Peterson and Schottenheimer, bolstered by the likes of talent evaluators Whitey Dovell, who died in 1992, and Lynn Stiles, Mark Hatley and Terry Bradway and a crew of able assistants in the player personnel department, made numerous shrewd acquisitions through trades and free agent signings—starting with Dan Saleaumua the first year, and on to big-play names like safety Mark Collins,

cornerback James Hasty, tackle Joe Phillips on defense, and fullback Kimble Anders, tight end Keith Cash and quarterback Steve Bono on offense. Further, the Chiefs attracted starters Ricky Siglar for the interior offensive line, Tracy Simien at linebacker, safety Brian Washington, and punter Louie Aguiar.

Carl Peterson.
(© Young Company)

The inaugural Carl & Marty draft produced gems at linebacker in Derrick Thomas (first round, fourth pick out of Alabama) and receiver in Robb Thomas (sixth round, Oregon State). Later significant draftees included second-rounder Tim Grunhard at center from Notre Dame, Dave Szott at guard from Penn State (7th round), Tim Barnett at wide receiver from Jackson State (3rd), first-rounder Dale Carter from Tennessee at cornerback, Will Shields at guard from Nebraska (3rd), and the sterling group from 1994—running backs Greg Hill from Texas A&M (1st) and Donnell Bennett from Miami (2nd), and wide receivers Lake Dawson from Notre Dame and Chris Penn from Tulsa (both in the 3rd). Other draft choices became starters, albeit briefly (tackle Derrick Graham, linebacker Percy Snow, defensive back Charles Mincy, and the Chiefs held high hopes for several who came through the 1996 draft (safeties Jerome Woods and Reggie Tongue, defensive end John Browning and linebacker Donnie Edwards).

"Finds" became a trademark of the Schottenheimer/Peterson regime. Free agents such as Tracy Simien, Willie Davis, and Sean LaChapelle became regulars. And, in another way through clever background checking and anticipation, Tamarick Vanover from the CFL was selected in the draft while other teams were looking the other way.

Simien joined the Chiefs on the practice squad after being cut by two teams. He entered the NFL as a free agent with the Steelers out of Texas Christian in 1989. The Steelers and Saints both released him. The Chiefs put him on their practice

Marty Schottenheimer displays his competitiveness in the heat of battle. (© Young Company)

squad in 1990. In 1991 he played for the Montreal Machine in the fledgling World League, where, at middle linebacker, he gained some notice as "Mr. Helmet Cam"—the first to place a mini-camera in his helmet so television viewers could see every play coming right at them. He advanced into the Chiefs' lineup that fall and led the team in tackles four straight seasons, 1992-95.

Davis was a speedy wide receiver out of Central Arkansas whom the Chiefs invited in as a free agent to join the developmental squad. "He told us to go jump in a lake unless we gave him a bonus," said Denny Thum, assistant general manager who negotiates contracts. Finally, Davis gave in, and he spent not one, but two years with the practice group. He also agreed to a season in the WLAF to gain experience, joining the Orlando Thunder in '92. That fall he earned a start in mid-season, and over the next $3^{1}/_{2}$ seasons gained more than 3,000 yards receiving for the Chiefs before leaving as an unrestricted free agent for $6 million over four years with the Oilers.

Another wide receiver, LaChapelle, didn't stick with the Rams in '94 after they drafted him in 1993 in the fifth round. He'd been out of football a season when the Chiefs tried him out in February of '95 and signed him, but he was cut from training camp after hurting his back in a preseason game. He went to

the World League, became its Most Valuable Player while leading the Scottish Claymores to the championship with record receiving yardage. The Chiefs signed him again, he was cut again, but joined the team for the fifth game, made eight starts, and caught 27 passes for 422 yards and two TDs.

Vanover was a prize catch (and catcher) in the Canadian Football League in 1994 after playing just two years at Florida State. The Chiefs, following up on some diligent detective work, determined that his CFL team, the Las Vegas Posse, would be defunct and that he wouldn't fit under the salary cap of the team that had his rights, the Winnipeg Blue Bombers. So, the Chiefs drafted him in the third round; other teams ignored him, believing he wouldn't be signable. He immediately became one of the most exciting players to wear the Chiefs uniform, as a kick returner and receiver.

The punctuation marks to all the maneuvering, to the championship-targeted buildup, were marquee names, present and future Hall of Famers—center Mike Webster, Allen at running back, and Montana to steer the drive to the top that fell a tad short before Webster and Montana retired.

"We won't be satisfied, and our jobs won't be completed, until we get there and win it," Peterson said at the conclusion of the 1996 season, his words pointed directly at the Super Bowl. As the 25th season at Arrowhead fell silent so unexpectedly and, in many ways, inexplicably, fans wondered for a month or so whether the era had also come to an end without the job being completed.

Even though Schottenheimer had a contract running through 1997, rumors flew that he would depart, flying in the face of Lamar Hunt's calm remarks to the contrary. Hunt also said that the variety of speculation about Peterson's standing held no credibility, and sure enough, in January a new contract for Peterson kept the era alive, if not totally well. And each head of state, owner and president/GM and coach, assured their constituency that the club was forging ahead full-bore toward the coveted grand prize.

They wasted no time with the promise of a new quarterback, with acquiring what Schottenheimer referred to as "playmakers," with making some changes in the coaching staff, and with declaring a renewed sense of urgency about the draft and squad selection.

Peterson could look back on the years with pride and satisfaction as he sat behind his desk in his Arrowhead office during the 25th anniversary season. He built on what was already established.

"One of the smartest things Kansas City did," Peterson began, "was let each franchise operate its own facility, and that instilled pride in ownership. The condition and image of Arrowhead Stadium is a credit to the people in operations through the years, and the guiding hand of Jack Steadman."

This compared, for example, to Peterson's experience in Philadelphia, where he coached with the Eagles during 1977-79, and where he helped build the USFL Philadelphia Stars during the '80s. The city owns Veterans Stadium, "…and that's a different mentality," Peterson said. "Here, everybody takes pride—the plumbers, the painters, the groundskeepers, everyone."

With Schottenheimer and his staff in place (he brought seven assistants from Cleveland) the task began to construct a playoff team and provide top entertainment value, with fan satisfaction as the operative words. "There are only so many discretionary sports fan satisfaction dollars, and we can't ever forget that sports is in the entertainment business," Peterson said. "It's dinosaur thinking that if you win, fans will automatically come."

Peterson assembled a larger organization than most NFL teams have, including 28 fulltime persons in stadium operations. He hired Tim Connolly, and the immediacy focused directly on one objective: Arrowhead comfort and ease of use and fun, fun, fun for the fan. The front office was bent on innovation, rooted in Peterson's experiences in Philadelphia competing with pro baseball, hockey and basketball, plus Atlantic City just 90 miles away. ("We had to get people to come see something called pro football in the spring.")

So, for many months, Arrowhead played host not just to football action on the field, but off the field to focus groups of fans, to demographic studies, to seminars in the Arrowhead Club—a plethora of internal activity to supplement the No. 1 goal: a strong product on the field.

The Chiefs Club Red Coaters booster group of ticket sellers was revitalized. A fan assistance plan was implemented. The Chiefs Ambassadors formed, spearheaded by the late Buck Buchanan and comprising all former Chiefs players who desire to foster good relations with the fan constituency; they gather in a huge tent with guests on the southwest side of the stadium before every game. "We needed to connect the greatness of the Chiefs' past with the future," Peterson said. "I can't say enough about Buck Buchanan in helping that come about."

Aggressively, the new regime pursued that future, centering on a belief that major change would be very positive. The attitude that permeated had to be fumigated. Some changes in the new regime met with frowns and bewilderment—the retiring of the horse mascot, moving training camp away from Kansas City, shifting radio broadcasts to an FM rock station. "Some changes were difficult, because people were so accustomed to certain things," Peterson said.

People loved War Paint, the horse who trotted onto the field after Chiefs scores. He was put to pasture. Connolly examined all the machinations of Sundays at Arrowhead, and many new ideas were infused into the entertainment package, including the new mascot, K.C. Wolf, Connolly's brainstorm intended to bring a "big furry, lovable animal that appealed to family values." The creativity of Connolly and his right-hand marketing man, Phil Thomas, and public relations director Bob Moore moved rapidly straight to the heart of the matter, which was to raise the spirit of the ticket-buyer.

Training camp moved from Liberty, where Chiefs fans could drift out during the dog days of summer and see what was in store. Peterson, amidst a smattering of boos, moved camp River Falls, Wis. Our training camp was not creating a competitive advantage," Peterson pointed out. "We moved to where there were four other NFL teams within two hours. It's helped us immensely. And 9,000 people show up for a scrimmage."

The people upstairs, with carte blanche endorsement from Peterson to go get 'em, invented new pregame and halftime pizzazz. They even created a new radio world. Peterson went FM, with 101 The Fox, and at the time that was something only a handful of teams had taken a chance on. It infused the radio team of Kevin Harlan (and later, Mitch Holthus), Len Dawson, Bill Grigsby, and Bob Gretz with a more energetic, contemporary backdrop before, during and after games, and throughout the week. And other radio stations created a whole radio band of Chiefs voices, day and night—Derrick Thomas, Tim Grunhard, Joe Phillips, Carl Peterson among them, giving exposure to every facet of the Chiefs organization. Marcus Allen took it a step further with a wildly popular, live audience weekly TV show.

The club became intensely interactive with the fans in every way, writing to them, calling them, keeping them informed of every nuance of the new regime. There were no bombastic promises. In fact, the first TV ads were in black and white, shot in the weight room beneath Arrowhead Stadium, depict-

ing players working out to the backdrop of a theme, "No Slogans, No Promises—Just Hard Work!"

This, Peterson believed, would suit the psyche of the Show-Me State and surrounding metropolitan area that had been through five coaches in 11 years. They didn't want talk, they wanted action. "No flash right off the bat. Do it," Peterson said, "and do it again, and then I believe you, you've got me." His foresight was good. Quickly, the stadium went from the bare bones of his 1988 visit to waiting lists for season tickets and suites.

And by then, the do-it presentation was buffered by the stated goal of reaching the Super Bowl within five years. Boldly stated. The plan stretched on, past the fifth year, past the 25th year of Arrowhead, and the renewed Peterson/Schottenheimer combination surged forward, undaunted by the bumps in the road. They had paved a road that was mostly smoothe to travel, and trips that were mostly pleasurable to look back on …

Peterson reflected during the silver anniversary season on his favorite among many, many treasured events of his first eight seasons, and two surfaced above all others, the same two that most regulars arrive at quickly in any litany of great Arrowhead moments: Monday night against the Bills, and Montana against the 49ers.

"I don't know that I ever have experienced anything like Monday Night Football with the Bills in town, or ever will again," he said, his emotions on his sleeve. "It was riveting. It still makes the hair on the back of my neck stand up just thinking about it."

The ABC Monday Night crew hadn't been attracted to Arrowhead since 1983, so the thrill had accumulated eight years of dust when Buffalo came to town Oct. 7, 1991. The place was packed and aromatic and juiced and seemingly louder than ever, howling in delight at a 33-6 whacking of the Chiefs' former coach's team that was a Super Bowl fixture.

"There was an electricity in the air created by the fans," Peterson said, "like none I'd known. And I've been to full-house Rose Bowls, Super Bowls, the biggest and the best. Our team was so ready to play"—he spoke each word with emphasis— "that I knew, just KNEW, there was no way we were going to lose."

The Joe–San Francisco game is a no-brainer on the memory scale. The acquisition of Montana in 1993 and the team's 11-5 season that carried all the way to the AFC championship game (before Buffalo

butted in) stirred the masses, and 1994 couldn't have begun at home with any more passion. After an opening road victory, the Chiefs played host to Joe's former mates, and beat them 24-17.

"I was so happy for him," Peterson said. "There wasn't anybody who wanted anything more than I wanted for him to beat the 49ers."

Otherwise, Peterson simply loves the thought of most any Sunday (or Monday or Thursday) at the home of the Chiefs. "I just love seeing the fans get excited." The 1996 Packers game on Nov. 10, televised by the Fox Network, provided a capsule microcosm of what Peterson means. "They (Fox) do things different from the other networks on the introduction of lineups, and I wanted our team on the sideline for the Air Force fly-over, which was against their policy. But I put my foot down; I told them, 'You're not going to take that experience away from them…you can accommodate us, NBC does.' They did, and it was stupendous."

In summary of the facelift and, most noticeably, the spirit lift at Arrowhead Stadium as the pages turned on the 20th Century, Peterson noted, "This has been a lot of fun. Our plan was to make coming to a Chiefs game such an enjoyable experience you would always want to come back. And the fans in this city have reassured me that it's a great sports town. There simply are no fans like our Midwest fans.

"The excitement has climbed steadily. Our first playoff games (at Arrowhead). Becoming attractive to Monday Night Football again. In the 1980s we had one Monday night game, and in the '90s we've had 13. That's a flattering compliment to what's happening at Arrowhead Stadium. As a result, the Chiefs are third in total NFL merchandise sales.

"All those things are nice, but you know, more than anything else I love the college atmosphere—and that's what we have at Arrowhead. People plan their pregame cookouts months ahead, and they come dressed and ready to help us win. Our players love to play in this place. And our opponents hate to play here. That's the best thing you can say about Arrowhead Stadium."

The Montana Caper

One of the most exciting moments in Arrowhead history was the arrival of Joe Montana. It changed the face of the Chiefs forever, in marketing, in national and international attention and favor and in the belief system on the field.

The circumstances of the signing of Montana became one of the all-time highlights for an entourage of Chiefs administration that participated, especially Denny Thum, the executive vice-president and assistant general manager in charge of contract negotiations and salary cap monitoring. Thum was part of the Arrowhead scene all but its first two years, and he put together scores of deals with Chiefs draftees, free agents, and key players whom they retained. This one was extra special.

"It came together on napkins and scratch paper at Harry Starker's on the Plaza," Thum said. "We had flown Joe and Jennifer in on a private jet belonging to a local company (Lockton Insurance), and we had gone through dessert when the possibility started to become a reality."

Team owner Lamar Hunt was part of the Chiefs administration team and attended the recruiting dinner. Montana and his agents, Peter Johnson and former Chiefs lineman Tom Condon of IMG, also were surrounded by Thum, General Manager Carl Peterson, Coach Marty Schottenheimer, VP of Player Personnel Lynn Stiles, and one of Montana's mentors during glory days in San Francisco, offensive coordinator Paul Hackett, brand new to the staff at the time.

After dessert Peterson, Thum and the two agents adjourned to a private room. "Once we were able to negotiate within our salary parameters," Thum reflected, "it got to a point of,

Executive Vice President, Assistant General Manager, Denny Thum.

'Hey, this could happen.' We did final tabulations, as they related to the (salary) cap, and the agents came back with, 'If you can do this, Joe Montana will become a Chief.' We ordered up champagne."

As a bottle of bubbly arrived from the private reserve in the wine cellar, the wives, who had been milling around during the negotiations, wondered aloud what was up. The husbands' smiles and a toast let them know what Carmen Policy, the man who operated the San Francisco 49ers, soon would know: without question, Joe Montana would grace Arrowhead in a Chiefs uniform for two or three years (it turned out to be two).

The signing was a coup for Peterson and Thum–a testament to their considerable persuasiveness and negotiating skills–because Montana had other possibilities to consider, such as the Arizona Cardinals. Instead, he added a distinctive Hall of Fame flavor to an already star-studded history.

Joe Montana

Coming to Arrowhead. (left to right) Jennifer Montana, Joe Montana, Carl Peterson

Just as he had turned the National Football League upside-down with 49ers Fever on the way to four Super Bowl championships, quarterback Joe Montana turned Kansas City upside-down simply by his presence after he signed on with the Chiefs in 1993. He played but two seasons for the Chiefs, foregoing a final option year on his contract and retiring April 18, 1995, as the NFL's No. 1 all-time passer.

In assaying the most memorable games played at Arrowhead, everybody had Sept. 11, 1994, high atop their list, a 24-17 Chiefs victory over the 49ers with Montana at the throttle against his former team.

Montana shared a few of his thoughts about his days at Arrowhead, especially that game against San Francisco that attracted worldwide media:

"Everybody makes such a big deal out of the game when we beat the 49ers my second year (24-17). It didn't seem like that big a deal to me, because it was so early in the season (the home opener, second game). It's just that I was playing against my old teammates and good friends."

Public relations director Bob Moore said it seemed "like a trillion" requests for media passes were forthcoming for that game, and the press box bulged with 400-plus after 100 folding chairs were put in place. Another 100 photographers and TV personnel were on the field. "The amount of focus on us nationally, and even internationally, during the Joe Era was phenomenal," Moore said.

"He was the second-most popular athlete in America only to Michael Jordan. Media came from virtually every continent—we had reporters and TV crews from Australia, Europe, Japan, Central America, Canada, China—and it was always about Joe. A crew from Guam for a fitness show even shot a feature of Joe working out, and he really wasn't even much of a workout guy."

Montana accepted the fever graciously, and, in typical fashion, he downplayed the special aura of "the" game, his match against former mates. "My memories, both as an opponent and in a Chiefs uniform, are more general than about specific games," he said. "The fans at Arrowhead are consistently high above any place else in terms of decibels. Marty Schottenheimer told me when I came here, 'Whatever I tell you about how loud it gets, it will be more.' He was right. That was the most exciting thing about playing here. You could always count on the electricity being there, as an opponent and as a Chief. I get goose bumps thinking about it still."

He praised Chiefs fans in another regard, too. "One thing I always found is that the Kansas City fans showed a lot of respect to the other team's players," Montana said. "It wasn't like other places, where they throw things and yell, 'You stink.' The Chiefs have great fans who make you feel good."

Sometimes they created headaches for the club. Moore recounted some sticky situations. Once a woman at training camp in River Falls, Wis., requested that Montana autograph some beer cans. "We had to tell her, no, ma'am, that would not be appropriate," Moore said. "Another woman called on game day before we played the Raiders in 1993 (Oct. 3), crying, hysterical, explaining that her husband had been cremated and she wanted Joe to come over and sign his urn. After she hung up, the guy's mother called, begging for the same thing.

"There was a constant crowd out front that would show up to have him sign things—everything imaginable, like lamps." The club beefed up with extra security to keep fans from sneaking in on non-game days during the week and stealing stuff from Joe's locker. "You'd be amazed at things that showed up for sale," Moore said, "like his shoes did one time. Some fans think they're entitled to anything and everything."

While Joe wowed the fans on the field and they clamored for him off the field, his wife, Jennifer, carved her own niche in their consciousness, too—as a television feature reporter. She participated in locally-produced pregame TV specials, among a variety of special assignments.

"At Arrowhead before home games you could always find several amazing tailgate parties," she said. "I remember one with a roasted pig. The TV was the fun part for me as Joe's wife, because it helped relieve the pressure."

She will never forget the 49ers game, she said. (Get in line, Jennifer.) "That was one of the largest tailgate parties ever. It was great to feel all the support for Joe, because after he was separated from San Francisco it was never quite the same back there. Montana Country became Young Country. So, Kansas City gave us a weekend we could never forget."

Both Montanas said they got a large kick out of the little town of Ismay, Montana, population 93, that, as part of a radio station's brainstorm, renamed itself "Joe." Virtually the whole town flew to Kansas City for a game. It was the home of a couple of performers who made the Rodeo Hall of Fame, and Montana declined to have his photo made with them because he didn't want to detract from their achievements. "They were the greatest people," Montana said. One of them, upon bidding him adieu, said, "If you ever go up our way, let us know when you're passing through so we can make the bed for you."

Joe Montana, looking toward Canton.
(photo by Tim Umphrey)

Jennifer Montana observed, "The adulation is so widespread and so overwhelming sometimes, I really don't understand where it all comes from. But that, having a town named for you, was really quite an honor."

She summed up their brief, two-year stay in the Chiefs fold: "We had such a good time, and it truly was sad to go. Our neighborhood was so pleasant, and we made outstanding friends. Often I have wished that Joe had had a couple of more years left."

Marcus Allen

Marcus Allen. (© Young Company)

Marcus Allen arrived in 1993, marching stealthily toward NFL records even though he had been displaced repeatedly in the lineup the previous four years with the Raiders, and he became the Chiefs' Most Valuable Player in two of his first four seasons.

As he added touchdowns and yardage in moving up the all-time charts, he developed a keen relationship not only with teammates in Kansas City, but also with the multitudinous fans who packed Arrowhead Stadium and chanted his name, "Mar-cus, Mar-cus!"

Whenever the Chiefs moved near the enemy goal line during Allen's five-year regime, anticipation mounted. The fans knew what was coming. The opposition knew. And the Chiefs' coaching staff was fully aware that the opposition knew. But so what? It was virtually unstoppable. Allen either took the handoff and cut or dived into the end zone, or he faked it to set up another play. One teammate observed, "We'll never know how many touchdowns Marcus could have scored had he played full-time all those years for the Raiders, and if he hadn't unselfishly asked Coach Schottenheimer to use him as a decoy to open things up for someone else to score."

Contemplating his playing days at Arrowhead, both as an archrival Raider and as a Chiefs staple, Allen expressed an appreciation for the roar that Chiefs fans could muster to fill the place with cascading sound. "The crowds really get into it there," he said. "A large crowd always stimulated me. So I can't think of a better place to play, with all due respect to several other cities with good fans.

"In Kansas City they are intelligent enough, sophisticated enough to know when to raise their voices to the heavens. At the same time I have to say that as loud as it is, once I'm lined up for a play I don't hear the noise. It's more when I'm standing on the sideline."

Back when Allen played for the Raiders, the first thing he noticed about visiting Arrowhead was how cold it could get. Keep in mind that this comes from a guy who grew up in San Diego, and attended the University of Southern California, where he earned the Heisman Trophy as the nation's most outstanding player.

"The first game I ever played here with the Raiders was the first place I ever played where it was actually cold," Allen recalled. "I stood too close to the heater on the sideline, and one of my shoes melted down. I gave myself a hotfoot."

Warmth of another sort, an outpouring from fans, permeated Allen's days in a Chiefs' uniform after he'd spent 11 years with the team they hated most. "Kathryn (his wife) and I probably received more out of the move to Kansas City than its fans did. I feel wealthy from what they've given to me, in terms of respect.

"I believe respect for human beings is the most important thing. Coming from a negative situation (Raiders), anybody would feel the need to be wanted."

As he wound down his career in 1997, he was not simply wanted by fans at Arrowhead, they clamored for him . . . and his trademark dives over the top of blocking linemen and would-be tacklers into the end zone.

(Photo by Gary Carson)

(Photo by Jim Langlois)

Chapter 7
The Fans

"... You've always made game day come alive.

—Lamar and Norma Hunt, in a letter to Chiefs season ticket holders, 1996

HICH CAME FIRST, THE FOOTBALL TEAM OR the fans? That's neither a trick question nor a philosophical conundrum in Chiefs history. The fans came first, both times—when the team moved to Kansas City from Dallas, and when the team moved to Arrowhead Stadium from Municipal Stadium. A phenomenal season-ticket

base, grounded in a support group of legendary proportion, the Wolfpack, preceded the Chiefs' first game at both sites.

The lowest the all-season-we're-there-behind-you core ever dipped was 24,610, so even the lean years had their faithfuls in droves. By the end of the 25th season at Arrowhead (the 34th season of the Chiefs), there were about 21,000 season ticket accounts amounting to some 72,000 tickets, leaving a trail on a waiting list of more than 4,000 names wanting more than 10,000 more seats! In 1995 ticket buyers came from 41 states plus Puerto Rico. And coming out of the 1996 silver anniversary season, despite the disappointment of missing the playoffs, the renewal rate on the 72,000-plus season tickets was 99.4 percent!

Hence the theme of a commemorative gift package to long-standing season ticket holders in the 25th year of Arrowhead: "It's been a great ride, and you've been with us all the way." Chiefs fever created a monster.

Or, actually, in this case the monster created itself. On Chiefs game day, the migration to the Harry S. Truman Sports Complex resembles some kind of mass evacuation process, except that everybody is converging into one place rather than getting out. (The getting out is something else entirely, a supreme test of patience and driving nerves.) "It's like the Oklahoma land rush when the gates open," owner Lamar Hunt described the scene. "They start staking their turf, and the party is on."

The team was Super Bowl sensational before it arrived at Arrowhead, and Chiefs football had old Municipal Stadium creaking at the seams. But even though the team showed signs of wear in tapering off from championship performance, the spirit of what preceded 1972 brought an even larger swirl of activity to the parking lots of Arrowhead, which spilled over into the seats at game time. (Although... an amazing number of fans who can't get tickets will pay the parking fee, set up shop with food and TV, and watch the game outside the stadium walls, soaking in the ambient crowd roars while catching the action from Mitch and Lenny and Grigs and Gretz with the TV sound turned down.)

As a result, you get a massive combination of bazaar and bizarre. You get the regulars who

A variety of fan headgear... (© Young Company)

arrive early by camper, van, motor home, pickup truck, bus, moving van, bicycle and, oh yeah, car and they stake out spots they have used for years, creating a little neighborhood. They raise flag poles—J.D. Martin's of Lenexa is 52 feet high, the unofficial champion of flagpoles—and they fly the colors of the Chiefs, the United States, and sometimes their favorite college team, to boot. They cook and mingle and whoop. They paint and decorate their vehicles, their bodies, and, thus, the day.

The Zamora family is an example. West lot, about midway deep in the center, flag flying with a 'Z' marks the spot. They started the ritual in the mid-'70s. Food, music, fellowship, and eventually

football. Tickets are pooled so many different people get to experience the event.

On the north side between Arrowhead and Kauffman Stadium, the parking lots become Tent City. Sponsors set up for clients, replete with TV sets, bands, and plenty of booze and schmooze. On the opposite side, boosters mingle with former Chiefs in an "alumni" tent. Individuals and clusters move about constantly around the stadium, like ants aswirl, hawking tickets, seeking autographs or a brush with somebody famous like an ex-player or, say, owner Lamar Hunt who often takes a stroll through the pregame potpourri to shake hands and hear what people like and dislike.

...appears all across Arrowhead.
(© Young Company)

Chiefs fight song then boom! … Go Chiefs! (photo by Tom Mitchell)

I now pronounce you Chiefs fans. The happy couple Barbara and Mike Shaw with Lamar Hunt.

and they suddenly said, 'That's our flag.' They were up there surveying their own flag. That added to the joy of the moment."

Beyond, in the same east parking lot, a band struck up some lively, rockin' music. After a bit, the band started the haunting strains of the song to which Chiefs fans do The Tomahawk Chop, borrowed from Florida State University lore. As Hunt observed, fans strolled by or gathered around, hummed the tune, did The Chop. At the end, band leader Dave Shipman set off a fuse that ignited some powder and sent a large puff of smoke exploding into the sky. Happens every Sunday, or Thursday, or Monday, day or night— whatever the schedule requires.

Some fans take their emotional outpouring to great length. Like Arrowman. He is Monte Short. Seemingly, otherwise, a normal guy from Independence, Mo., a homebuilder by profession. On Chiefs game days he wears the opposing teams jersey and cap, and has arrows protruding from every part of his head and upper body. Is he ill? Yes, clearly; he caught the fever in 1970 when he lied to the school nurse at his high school in 1970, saying he was sick so he could attend the Chiefs Super Bowl parade. Arrowman first appeared at the Steelers game Oct. 25, 1992, and grew from there as he donned padding and Chiefs pants for protection against locals who didn't get the joke. Souvenir seekers deplete his supply of about six dozen arrows by game's end. Hunt has joined Arrowman on occasion with his regular entourage, all of whom wear costumes prepared by Short and his wife, Stacie.

Other exhibitionist sorts, although not as elaborate as Arrowman (who sports upward to $300 worth of jersey and arrows every game), also stand out in the crowd. Such as the bare-bellied men of Section 123 who paint bullseyes on their bods with the enemy insignia in the center and an arrow sticking out. For the most part, though, the smattering of paint-smeared or wild-costumed fans is minute compared to the long-standing ticketholders who are there year after year, through thick and thin, filling every seat.

In 1996, the silver anniversary season, Hunt had his car towed because it didn't have the proper parking pass displayed in the window. He attended a wedding in a tent outside the stadium two hours before game time against The Pack from Green Bay, in which the bride wore a hand-made dress of crimson-and-gold adorned with Chiefs insignias. One guy witnessed it wearing a cheese-head.

Before another game Hunt was circling the club level deck on the east side when he encountered a couple admiring a tall, tall flagpole in the parking lot. "It must have been 50 feet high with a telescoping mechanism, flying a humongous flag in Chiefs colors," Hunt said. "I commented on it,

This small city that regenerates every game day shakes the earth with its crescendo once game time approaches. Dan Dierdorf declared on a Monday Night Football telecast what many have said repeatedly through the ages: "This is the loudest outdoor stadium in the NFL." Bill Grigsby on the Chiefs radio network once said, "Folks, you wouldn't want the Wolfpack against you. It's mean. It will devour you whole."

Marty Schottenheimer, a veteran of many venues, said there is none better (or worse, if you're the visiting team) than Arrowhead. "I experienced all of the toughest places to play—many years of the Dog Pound in Cleveland (when he coached the Browns)… the closed end of the field in Denver where the visitors come out to the field… but there's no place any tougher than Arrowhead Stadium," he said. "It must be louder than any place in the world… clearly, at least the loudest non-domed stadium."

Never minimize what that means to the home team. Schottenheimer again:

"There's no question that when you have the kind of crowd at Arrowhead Stadium we do, it's a major positive. That's absolutely clear. I'm sure it works against you (opponents), and I've been fortunate not to have been in those situations. It's hard to hear, so it affects players' concentration. You can practice with noise in the background that is louder than what you'll get at a game, which is nervewracking in a small facility, but when the game starts all you can do when you come into a hostile environment like this is play well early enough that it dampens the crowd's enthusiasm. I don't recall that happening here. I remember it once, for example, at Denver when the crowd was going nuts after one of their touchdowns. Tamarick Vanover ran back the ensuing kickoff for a touchdown, and you could hear a pin drop at Mile High. I'm glad there is no noise rule at Arrowhead."

Additionally, apart from the madding crowd that crawls and sprawls into and around Arrowhead on game day, there are countless legions like Mary Cain. In her 80s after a long career as a military secretary in Germany, Tripoli and Korea, Mary became a rabid follower of team fortunes from her home every week after retiring in 1975. She placed a small Chiefs flag out by a tree in her front yard on game days and soaked in the action by TV and radio. "Very faithfully," she said. "I'm a loyal Chiefs fan." She wrote to Derrick Thomas after reading about his search for his father's name on the Vietnam Memorial wall, and Mary delighted when she met a neighbor who was Carl Peterson's administrative assistant, Barbara Harrington, and received a tour of the entire stadium. Fans like that, many who never attend a game, contribute to the phenomenon of Chiefs football.

They are what Arrowhead is mostly about. Sure, the team, too. If there's no team, there's no crowd; chicken and the egg, yadda yadda. But listen to the description of the one guy most closely associated with Chiefs football on the field, Len Dawson, who followed his 14 years of playing for the team with a career in the broadcast booth on KMBC-TV Channel 9, HBO's "Inside the NFL," and the Chiefs radio network:

"It's that sea of red created by what the fans wear, and the noise, the deafening noise, that makes Arrowhead Stadium unique. And it creates a disadvantage for the opposition. The Chiefs, from day one, have been blessed with phenomenal fans."

(© Young Company)

Chapter 8
Staples of Arrowhead

(Lightfoot photo)

The Flyovers

The regular-season opener against the Dolphins in 1972 featured a sensational pregame treat, a flyover of military jets-and a tradition was born.

Lee Derrough, marketing director of Worlds of Fun then (a Hunt property), assisted this segment of the unveiling of Arrowhead by calling a buddy stationed with a squadron of fighter pilots and planes at the Lemoore Naval Air Station in California. The friend made it happen.

The plans were all set with the planes timed to be over the mass of people as close as possible to the end of the national anthem. Geared with a survival radio to communicate with the pilots, Derrough explained what unfolded that day, "I gave them a one-minute 'Go, you better be here.' They leveled off I-don't-know how-many miles out there and I could see them putting the juice to it. You could see the black smoke coming out of the tails of the planes.

Almost simultaneously, Derrough noticed some company in the air space overhead.

"I noticed at the time that there was one of those bi-planes pulling a "Eat at Joe's" banner over the stadium and I said, "You better look out for these guys. And I'll be darned if they didn't go under him."

The pilots flew to thunderous approval from the Arrowhead crowd. Since then, the flyovers have provided some of the most memorable moments at Arrowhead.

From the fighters during their annual flyover to the Stealth (pictured above, top), Arrowhead fans have seen a wide range air displays over the stadium before kickoff. (Photo by Chris Dennis)

Staples of Arrowhead

The Tunnel

The scene gets wild along the edges of the tunnel-both inside and outside of Arrowhead where players enter the stadium and take the field. Streams of fans line the edges, leaning, reaching and clamoring either to get the attention of a favorite Chief, or to berate a favorite opponent.

Real Grass

With George Toma, the best groundskeeper in the world, calling Kansas City home, the question before 1994 lingered: How could the most beautiful stadium in the NFL be laid out with an artificial playing surface?

That question was put to rest when the Chiefs announced they were going to a natural surface. Chip Toma, George's son, was the Director of the Truman Sports Complex landscaping at the time before the NFL beckoned, so Andre Bruce is now the head groundskeeper.

(© Young Company)

"It's a big challenge, myself and the rest of the crew were looking for because on artificial turf you only had to do certain things like paint it and it's pretty much like your carpet at home. You vacuum it," explained Bruce from his Arrowhead office. "With grass there's a bigger challenge because this is something that's alive and you have to keep it alive by fertilizing, by spraying it when it needs it and by watching it every day."

The Mural

Inside the main entrance, to the Chief's offices a massive work of art covers the wall behind the switchboard operator's desk.

Nationally renowned sports artist John Martin, with some help from his friends, constructed the two-story mural that is one of the unique works of art in any stadium.

"The main construction of it is wood, which is oak, solid oak with a walnut finish," said Martin. "It is also made up of materials such as masonite and actual cowhide leather that we were able to get from a local leather company. Then it was woodburned, sanded and leather stained."

Martin worked for three months with carpenters from "Display Studio," a company which cut the woodwork and put up the scaffolding. Down the stretch, Martin, who partnered with the Chiefs while with an advertising firm ("Kaine, Martin, Harmon and Peterson"), recruited his colleagues at the firm to help put the finishing touches on the mural.

"We were known as a total service agency and there is a real prime example of how it was. We all pitched in on a lot of things," said Martin, who believes the mural is so sturdy that it's likely stronger than the elevator shaft behind it.

(photo by Gary Carson)

Big Screen Video

Since the Chiefs first pre-season game against the St. Louis Cardinals in 1972, Bill Harmon has been the Director of Scoreboard Operations and he was presented with something no one in the world had ever operated before.

"Early on, it was a learning experience for everybody involved because it had not been done before," Harmon said, looking back retrospectively. "In those early days, we weren't nearly as quick as we are now."

From what appears to be a mini-television studio, Harmon and his staff of technicians mix the video, sound and graphics into what turns out to be a top notch presentation that keeps the fans informed and entertained. Through the years, the facilities have been updated, including the JumboTron screen in 1991.

"We remind ourselves constantly that we are not the show," said Harmon. "The show is the football game and what we do is make every effort to do what we can do to enhance that operation."

Former Chiefs play-by-play broadcaster Dick Carlson remembers how amazed he was when he walked into the room that serves as the central nervous system of the scoreboard operation.

"I remember how fascinated I was in 1972 as a radio and television broadcaster to walk into Master Control, he said." It was like walking into Master Control of a TV station. It was incredible."

"...and the Home of the (CHIEFS!)"

The word "Brave" is left to whoever sings the National Anthem, because Chiefs fans will get the last, thunderous word in before kickoff.

Many who made the trek to Houston for the season opener against the Oilers in 1996 sent a resounding cascade of sound through the Astrodome with a dose of the Arrowhead experience. The same vibrations rocked the Metrodome in Minneapolis when masses journeyed to watch the Chiefs take on the Vikings nine weeks later. "It was just like being at home," coach Marty Schottenheimer gushed afterward.

President/GM Carl Peterson addressed a Red Friday luncheon group preceding the 1996 home opener against the Raiders and he pointed out, "We all look forward, not only at Arrowhead, but on the road, too, to when we get to that stanza of the National Anthem, 'Home of the . . . CHIEFS!' Our players love it."

The Chop

A phenomenon from the Florida State college football and Atlanta Braves baseball scenes, "The Tomahawk Chop," grew wildly popular among Chiefs fans in the early '90s. The Northwest Missouri State University made an appearance at Arrowhead, and its band instructor came from Florida State. He had the band play the theme for fun during pregame warmups. Fans started emulating what they'd seen on TV, according to the marketing director at the time, Phil Thomas.

"Marty Schottenheimer told us after that game that the players really loved the Seminole song. So we had a tape cut by the (NWMS) band and sent the tape to all the other bands coming in, requesting that they learn it to play during our games. We also got the Pack Band to learn it."

Sometimes the players got into the habit, too, especially on defense-performing a perfunctory chop on cue when the haunting Seminole theme struck up after a big play.

"The Chop"
(© Young Company)

Jan and Nick kicking

Between them, during 22 Chiefs seasons at Arrowhead, Hall of Famer Jan Stenerud and Nick Lowery kicked 2,697 total points on 608 field goals and 873 extra points. They played in a combined 258 games at Arrowhead Stadium (including 66 preseason). Many of their kicks provided the victory margin in exciting finishes.

By the time the Chiefs moved into Arrowhead, fans knew Stenerud was extra special. They weren't so sure when the new kid arrived in his place. Well, one observer was besides coach Marv Levy. Clark Hunt, a son of the owner, proved prophetic during preseason camp of 1980. As a youth Clark worked at the camp, and one of his duties was to chart field goals during the kicking drills. Toward the end of camp he told a colleague, "Nick's going to beat out Jan."

Indeed, that happened, and fans soon discovered that Lowery was special, too. In just his second game he kicked a 57-yard field goal against the Seahawks. In 1985 he kicked the longest ever at Arrowhead, 58 yards against the Raiders on Thursday Night Football. At the outset, some teammates didn't warm to him because of their loyalty to Stenerud.

Lowery recalled, "Nobody ever owned up to it, but somebody filled my bed and chest of drawers in camp with fresh cow manure." Fortunately, his kicking prowess fertilized the Chiefs' offense as he accumulated 329 field goals and 1,466 points in 14 seasons. Among his many most memorable kicks, one held twofold special meaning to him-against Detroit on Oct. 26, 1980.

"National CBS telecast, tied 17-all, 5 minutes left. I'd hit a 52-yarder earlier in the game, and was 10-for-11, but hadn't had a moment of truth yet," Lowery said. "I stroked it through from 40, and we won 20-17. Jack Rudnay, our center and one of the guys who had been cool to me, hugged me on the sideline and said, 'You do your job, and I respect you for it.' That was a special moment for me. I got my first taste of involvment off the field from him. Every game Jack had a group around him known as Jack's Kids. He had this big, mean-guy presence, but he turned to a marshmallow in front of those kids. He was before his time in that regard, and I credit my community service work (Kick with Nick) to him as inspiration."

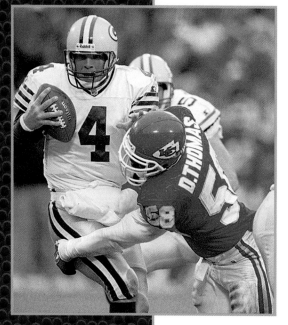

The Derrick Thomas Sack

Ever since he broke in with the Chiefs the same year Carl Peterson and Marty Schottenheimer arrived, it was apparent Derrick Thomas was going to make a major impact with the Chiefs. And no defensive play has generated more excitement year after year since his arrival than the Derrick Thomas sack. As Denver Broncos quarterback John Elway was reminded of early in the '96 season, Thomas is quick enough to pounce on the ball after a jarring hit.

Thomas' play through the years merited a historical announcement by Peterson on March 26, 1997:

"I'm very, very pleased to make the announcement that Derrick Thomas has signed a contract with the Kansas City Chiefs that will allow him to complete his entire NFL pro football career here with Kansas City."

In each of Thomas' first eight seasons with the Chiefs, he was selected to the Pro Bowl, two more times than the next closest honorees, Willie Lanier and Deron Cherry.

"He's the NFL's all-time leading sacker in his eight years, ahead of everybody else in the National Football League in that period. He's on a pace to set the all-time National Football League record," Peterson added at the news conference announcing Thomas' new contract.

The Baseball Swing

Neil Smith had been jokingly referred to by Derrick Thomas as "my partner in crime." Often, if Thomas didn't get through, Smith would have the goods on the opposing quarterback. They were a tandem for eight years before free agency caused the split.

But not forgotten will be the Neil Smith baseball swing, which made its debut on Monday Night Football in 1992 against the Raiders. It wasn't exactly an impromptu act.

"Martin Lawrence used to have a comedy show. How it came about was that Martin would say something very funny and, right after, he did a little swing," said Smith, reflecting after a pre-season practice one day. "I thought it was pretty cool."

It was no coincidence in the same year George Brett of the Kansas City Royals reached the elite distinction of collecting his 3,000th hit.

"I knew George had gotten his 3,000th hit and it was kind of exciting for him. I just went on to properly say that I'm going toward George Brett's 3,000 hits and this is the first one. I've got a long way to go, just jokingly," said Smith, who, by the way, started with a right-handed swing. Knowing that Brett was a left-handed hitter, Smith considered himself a switch-hitter, depending on which side of the quarterback he stood.

Neil Smith gets into the swing of it.
(© Young Company)

The Celebration

"I remember Elmo Wright dancing in the end zone," former Chiefs play-by-play man Dick Carlson said. "Elmo began the celebration when he got to the promised land. That's now just a way of life in professional football."

All post-play celebration dances, choreographed or spontaneous, can be attributed to wide receiver Elmo Wright, the Chiefs No. 1 draft choice in 1971. It actually started when Wright attended the University of Houston.

"I have to be honest, Hank warned me against it," Wright said, who now lives in Houston. He said the pros are not going to take it like the college players took it. But who was more of an individual than Hank Stram?"

Though not at the rate he scored touchdowns in college, Wright continued to dance in the pros. First, in the final season at Municipal Stadium, then in '73 and '74 at Arrowhead Stadium.

Arrowettes

Chances are, if you couldn't find your seat on opening day of Arrowhead, you would have been greeted by an Arrowette, the women ushers who made their debut with the opening of Arrowhead in '72.

Bob Wachter, who was the Chief's first employee when the Dallas Texans moved to Kansas City, was Director of Arrowhead Operations and one of his duties was to oversee the creation of the Arrowettes.

"Lamar Hunt liked the concept they used in Dallas with women ushers, so I spent several days observing how the Cowboys did it," Wachter said. "We started with a young lady named Sydna Bunton from Overland Park, who was Miss Teen-Age USA or something like that. And she was our poster girl."

Eventually, the Chiefs wound up hiring between 150 to 200 young women as Arrowettes.

Marty Schottenheimer Pep Talk

NFL Films captured the moment: Above the din at Arrowhead Stadium, Marty Schottenheimer, a coach known for his ability to motivate players, shouts some final words of encouragement to his team before kickoff.

One can safely wager that, somewhere in that pregame message, there was a mention of taking the game "one play at a time."

Staples of Arrowhead

Tailgating

Stake out a parking place, or four. Set up the grill, stoke the coals. The smoke signals soar, carrying their aromatic message: Game day at Arrowhead! As barbeque flavors and the sound of sizzle permeate the air, a unique fiefdom of fans forms on the paved lots and grassy knolls of the Truman Sports Complex.

From market surveys to discover what would make Arrowhead more user-friendly as the '90s dawned, Tim Connolly from the administration team discovered that fans yearned for a tailgate-party atmosphere. He directed the operations staff to make the area more amenable to becoming a giant barbeque pit.

They placed charcoal-disposal bins, aluminum can recycling bins, and the fans added the rest-tents, flagpoles, music, and red-theme regalia-to the pregame hullabaloo.

The only thing missing from these pages is the barbeque aroma (© Young Company)

"...A Beeeee-Yoo-Tee-Full Day"

Whether it be a warm, humid night for a pre-season game or a bitterly cold, gray day for an AFC playoff encounter in January, you couldn't convince Chiefs radio personality Bill Grigsby it was anything but "beeeee-yooo-tee-full."

Chiefs fans hear Grigby's proclamation on the Chiefs' radio pregame coverage. If you're looking for accurate weather conditions while stuck in traffic leading up to the stadium premises, forget it.

For *every* Chiefs home game, it's "beeeee-yooo-tee-ful," or least Grigsby will make you believe it is.

Tony and Patti DiPardo and the Pack Band

He turned 84 during the 25th anniversary season. He is known for his red trumpet and thumbs-up signal.

She has sung the National Anthem 29 times in the 25 years of Arrowhead and the Chiefs have only lost three of those contests.

Together, Tony and Patti DiPardo form a winning combination at Arrowhead with the support of an 11-person band. Tony's nephew, Tony III, joins in on electronics (sequencer). The others are: trumpeters Barry Springer, Craig Fuchs and Charlie Menghini (a former college professor in Olathe who, after he moved, flew in from Chicago to play at games); Steve Smith on sax, Mike Davis on piano, Kent Rausch on drums, John Isom on guitar and band technician Michael DiPardo, whom they call "Roadie."

"I loved it when Tony DiPardo would toot the 'Charge!'" said Len Dawson. Along with the "Charge" and "Go, Defense" bits, the band squeezes in "The War Chant."

"We just started doing the War Chant in 1992 with congas," said Tony DiPardo. "We had added those and rotatoms for more percussion. We had that beat going, and when I looked up into the lights, I saw a sea of red. Everybody was on their feet doing the chant. Ira Wilkes created a modern version of the war chant on bass, and we alternated between the traditional one and the modern one."

From 1983-88, DiPardo took a sabbatical as the team's music director due to health problems before he was asked back by Carl Peterson and Tim Connolly, whose research indicated the popularity of DiPardo in Kansas City.

"I told them, 'If you hire my daughter, you've got a deal.' They did. There's nothing better than a father-daughter combination," said DiPardo.

When the stadium opened, the band was known as the "TD Pack Band," but is more commonly referred to as the Pack Band.

*Tony DiPardo leads the Pack band and daughter Patti plays in the ensemble and occasionally sings the national anthem.
(© Young Company)*

Pre-game Introduction

After the opposition is introduced by P.A. announcer Dan Roberts with hardly any fanfare (unless it's a chorus of boos), the Chiefs cheerleaders and Red Coaters form a human tunnel leading out of the ramp from the dressing rooms. They take a 90-degree turn under the goal posts and extend through the end zone and onto the field for the Chiefs to run through upon introductions. All the while, the Pack Band highlights a guitar rift from "Sweet Child of Mine."

The color guard presents the flag before the National Anthem rings out. Marilyn Maye sang it at the first game at Arrowhead, returned on several other occasions including the 25th anniversary of the first rendition in the '96 season. Others who have taken the microphone are former Chiefs running back Theotis Brown, local singing standout Ida MacBeth and national recording artists such as Hank Williams Jr. and Billy Ray Cyrus.

With KC Wolf escorting a Jones Store Kid youth mascot, each team's captains meet at midfield for the coin toss. For a few seasons, the routine was followed by a video clip of "Cheers," when everyone in the bar was clapping and stomping in unison, a response after Roberts blares out, "Are you Ready?!" and the booming voice of Michael Buffer, "Let's get ready to rumble!" The familiar beat of the Rolling Stones' "Start Me Up" led to the opening kickoff and each kickoff thereafter throughout the day.

Color guard
(© Young Company)

(© Young Company)

The Red Coaters

One of the most anticipated moments in Arrowhead Stadium is the initial introduction of Chiefs players to the fans at Arrowhead Stadium. The photo above is the Chiefs first pre-season game against Buffalo and the introduction of new Chiefs quarterback, Joe Montana.

KC Wolf

Underneath that mascot suit is Dan Meers, who grew up in St. Charles, Mo. Before working at Arrowhead Stadium, Meers would pass by on the interstate on the way to either Lawrence, Manhattan or to Kemper Arena in Kansas City for the Big 8 tournament. As Truman the Tiger for the University of Missouri. He also has been Fredbird at St. Louis Cardinals baseball games.

KC Wolf has entertained the fans at Arrowhead and in the community since 1990. KC Wolf enhances the enthusiasm that is already carried through the stands.

"As a mascot, my job is to not only entertain, but also help create enthusiasm and excitement, Meers said. As far as Arrowhead goes, that makes my job real easy because of the fans in Kansas City and the whole atmosphere at Arrowhead Stadium."

Not all of his pre-game routines go off without a flaw, but you'd never know with Meers' ability to ad-lib. Once when KC Wolf was set to drive his ATV over the dummy wearing the opponents jersey, his four-wheeler died in the end zone.

"I couldn't get the thing started and got off and I was kicking the tire and acted like I was frustrated with it and just praying, 'Oh, let this bike start,'" Meers said. "Sure enough, I got back on and it started up again. I tell you, about 30 seconds in front of that many people seemed like 30 minutes."

During 60 minutes of football, you'll find KC Wolf in all corners of the stadium cavorting with fans.

(photo by Tim Umphrey)

(photo by Chris Dennis)

139

Staples of Arrowhead

Cheerleaders

High school cheerleaders were used in the inaugural season at Arrowhead. Later, from 1986-92, the cheerleaders were a mix of men and women. Today Chiefs cheerleaders are an exciting part of the Arrowhead atmosphere.

(© Young Company)   Through the years.   (photo by Gary Carson)

140

(© Young Company)   (photo by Tim Umphrey)

Chiefs Ambassadors

Honoring what they've given of their bodies on the field and to the community off the field, the Chiefs have maintained their link to the past with the Chiefs Ambassadors program. And you know what? They whoop it up now like any other fan.

The Kansas City Chiefs Ambassadors: Ted McKnight, Otis Taylor, Mike Bell, Ed Lothamer, Ed Budde, Charlie Getty, Walter White, Deron Cherry, Curtis McClinton, Jerry Cornelison, Dave Lindstrom, Bobby Bell, Larry Marshall, Bobby Ply, (not Pictured: Ken Kremer).

War Paint

War Paint was actually five different horses that took the field after a Chiefs' score. Bob Johnson, a rodeo cowboy, rode War Paint at the old stadium before carrying on the tradition at Arrowhead.

One time during the fourth pre-season game of the inaugural season, Johnson became sidelined after a ride aboard a War Paint he actually called "Trigger." Johnson injured an ankle while playing volleyball before that game on Sept. 2 against, the Dallas Cowboys. After a Chiefs score, War Paint, wearing rubber shoes because of the artificial turf, slipped and fell on the same ankle Johnson injured. It was broken, and so were his spirits that day when he couldn't ride anymore in the Chiefs' 20-10 win over the Cowboys.

Former Kansas City Star Chiefs beat writer Bill Richardson, who received the Tex Maule award in 1997 for special achievement in reporting pro football, said "The thing most striking about Arrowhead through the years is the pageantry and tradition. Things like the horse, War Paint, galloping around the field."

Bob Johnson aboard War Paint.

Chapter 9
What Next?
The Future at Arrowhead

AS AUGUST OF 1997, THE 25TH BIRTHDAY OF Arrowhead Stadium, approached, many curiosities arose about the immediate and long-term future of the home of the Chiefs. What next?

On the far horizon, the scene is lovely.

In an age when owners yank teams from communities—Oakland to L. A. and back, St. Louis to Phoenix, Cleveland to Baltimore, Houston to Tennessee—Kansas City has commitment. Lamar Hunt has never threatened to pull out, even through sticky renegotiations on a stadium lease, and it would be the shock of any century if he ever did.

The lease was redone through the year 2015. That locks the Chiefs in, and it's fine with Hunt. Annual funds are available to make improvements at Arrowhead, avoid dilapidation and keep it state of the art, based on a master plan.

Hunt has never looked back on his decision to move the Chiefs here. (He spends 30-40 nights per year in Kansas City as business here beckons, whether it is the Chiefs, Hunt Enterprises, or Hunt Sports, which primarily consists of Major League Soccer, the Kansas City Wizards and an MLS team in Columbus, Ohio, plus sports facility management.) In fact he always has looked ahead. To wit: reinvesting from Chiefs successes in Kansas City with theme parks, Worlds of Fun and Oceans of Fun (since sold) and other ventures.

With Arrowhead's next 19 years locked in for Chiefs action, the club focused its attention immediately in 1997 on finding healing solutions to rub on 1996's wounds. What next?

The ink on a newly-signed contract scarcely dry, president and general manager Carl Peterson joined head coach Marty Schottenheimer in loud and clear messages about the launching of the next generation of football talent, making several eyebrow-raising pronouncements:

Greg Hill was promoted to starting status ahead of future Hall of Famer Marcus Allen, whose blessing was attached. "Nobody will ever fully know how much Marcus has meant to Greg Hill, in terms of his patience and his development as a running back," Peterson said.

The ever-popular sackmeister, Derrick Thomas, was signed and removed from the free agent market, and he would move from linebacker to the line to enhance his opportunities to dump opposing quarterbacks.

Elvis Grbac would be the new quarterback hope for the Chiefs, displacing Steve Bono and becoming the third in succession and fourth overall to come from the San Francisco 49ers (following Steve DeBerg, Joe Montana, and Bono).

A large corps of new receivers joined the fold for Grbac to target–wide receiver Kevin Lockett and tight end Tony Gonzalez from the draft, and standout veterans Andre Rison and Brett Perriman at wideout and tight end Ted Popson through free agency. The retirement of stalwart left tackle John Alt after 14 years created a new look on the offensive line, and the newly-installed defensive alignment featured new faces, too, after the release of veterans such as Dan Saleaumua.

Any crystal ball discussion of what's next at Arrowhead Stadium always comes around to two popular and enticing subjects—a dome, and a Super Bowl. Don't count on either. Lack of one precludes the other.

Every now and then, over the last several decades, talk of a dome or other form of roof over Arrowhead arises from one source or another. Christopher Korth, a lawyer in Kansas City, wrote

to Lamar Hunt with a '90s kind of notion for overhead shelter, and at the time—1992 or so—Hunt did not discourage him. That's because Hunt never gave up on the idea of bringing a Super Bowl to the city, and he openly states that "without a dome, that is not within the realm of possibility." (On the day he was interviewed on the topic for this book, around Super Bowl time, Hunt asked rhetorically, "How'd you like to play the Super Bowl here today with the wind chill at minus-nine degrees?")

While Korth continues to pester folks with his grand scheme, Hunt said that the cost of putting a hat on Arrowhead would range upward to $100 million, and it would be very hard to justify. *Au contraire*, says Korth. Jeffrey Flanagan reported in *The Kansas City Star* (Jan. 29, 1997) that Korth's vision calls for selling the stadium name to a corporation, like the one in St. Louis, to underwrite part of the cost, and then to recuperate the rest by attracting the Super Bowl, Final Four and other major sporting events to the stadium.

Hunt said that as the '90s arrived the Chiefs and city officials ran an informal study on what would be required and what the plusses and minuses were to politicking for the Super Bowl site. "It was not going to work from a practical standpoint," Hunt said. The main drawback was that weather here would demand a dome, which would cost at least $75 million and probably more, or a sliding roof like Toronto's, which would push up through the $100 million barrier.

No matter how excellent the facilities are, Kansas City couldn't provide enough hotel space for the event.

"We have the stadium capacity for the Super Bowl, we have the ideal central location," Hunt said. "In our hearts, Arrowhead Stadium represents all that the Super Bowl symbolizes. Cities love the revenue that the game brings in over a two-week period. It's very desirable in many ways. But not practical."

So, what fans at Arrowhead could look forward to in the next quarter-century was the continued pursuit of the holiest of NFL grail, that slippery Super sensation, and the satisfaction of knowing that the rest of the football world will continue to envy, even copy that temple where Chiefs toil.

"We have a sports complex that every city in the NFL covets," Jack Steadman said. "Several, like the Giants, Lions, Saints, Dolphins, Panthers, all built new a new stadium with our footprint–suites, spacious club areas. But there's one major difference; they are pricing Joe Fan out of the game.

"We are still a Joe Fan city, and always intend to be."

(photo by Tim Umphrey)

Attendance

During each of the last three seasons the Chiefs led the entire National Football League in home attendance. During 1996—the 25th season at Arrowhead—Chiefs fans numbered an average of 76,327 a game, a total of 610,617 for eight home dates in the regular season. (This marked the fourth consecutive year that the Chiefs topped 600,000.) Add the two preseason games at home, and the Chiefs total jumped to 748,518 for 10 games.

This also became the fourth year in a row that the Chiefs led the NFL in total attendance for the regular season, home and away, with 1,073,522 attending the 16 games—the seventh consecutive season over 1 million.

As the first quarter of a century at Arrowhead concluded, the Chiefs had 50 consecutive sellouts (including three playoff games).

"We had two equal priorities when we came here," Carl Peterson, the Chiefs' president and general manager said. "They were to bring a championship to town, and to fill Arrowhead Stadium. Many people in this organization work very hard to achieve this (attendance) goal every year, and we are still working on getting that ring. We owe a large debt of gratitude to our fans, whom we believe to be the best in the NFL."